WHO WAKES
THE GROUNDHOG?

Ronald Rood

WHO WAKES THE GROUNDHOG?

Drawings by Carrye E. Schenk

W · W · Norton & Company · Inc ·

New York

Library of Congress Cataloging in Publication Data

Rood, Ronald N
   Who wakes the groundhog?

   1.   Seasons.   2.   Natural history.   I.   Title.
QH81.R738   574.1   71-139386
ISBN 0-393-08524-4

PRINTED IN THE UNITED STATES OF AMERICA

2 3 4 5 6 7 8 9 0

To Mrs. Karl Field—Henrietta, to her many friends—
who is as finely tuned to the outdoors as the living
things themselves, this book is gratefully dedicated.

To every thing there is a season,
and a time to every purpose under the heaven.
—*Ecclesiastes 3:1*

Contents

The Start of It All

THEY have little respect for our calendar, these living
things that share our land. Each one operates on a schedule of its own. Just as you're sure that the January woods
and fields have quieted down for the winter, your stroll
on a frozen pond reveals a turtle beneath the ice, plodding along in slow motion before burrowing into the
chilly mud. And even as you marvel at this discovery, you
get another surprise: out pops the first flower of spring.

Then, like as not, something stirs in the rattling
branches of the frozen trees overhead. It's a robin—a bird
you've always associated with spring, yet here it is nearly
three months ahead of time. It seems to shout, to a host
of slumbering plants and animals: "Get up! Time's a-wast-
ing!"

Nor is it alone on that wintry day. Its antics may be
noted by another bird: a great horned owl, already busy
with spring duties. To our minds this may be far from

nesting time, yet there she is—brooding two white eggs in
an old hollow tree, while the air snaps with the cold.

The first meal of the newly-hatched owlets may be the
remains of an unfortunate skunk, itself roused from winter sleep by the call to food and the search for fellowship
of the opposite sex. Snatched into the air by the owl, the
skunk probably trailed a cloud of ineffective spray as the
first five minutes away from its winter shelter turned out
to be the last five minutes of its life.

This June-in-January world is an intriguing place. For-
aging skunks and predatory owls, and flowers that bloom
in the snow are dramatic against the stark setting of winter. Yet each month—indeed, each day—of the year bears
evidence of some plant or animal that apparently cannot
wait for the season to come. And, each day, these living
things are counterbalanced by others that seem reluctant
to bid goodbye to the past.

Hence, the characters in this book. Just because the
four seasons begin on exact dates on our calendar is no
sign the living things of nature are bound by any such
timetable. Each travels at its own speed, finding its food,
seeking a mate, unfolding leaves, flinging seeds on the
wind in perfect timing with an age-old plan. Only recently have we begun to discover the workings of this
plan.

A special niche has been waiting for the early robin;
the bird fits the spot exactly. There's a reason why the
cricket sings in May but the grasshopper waits until July.
The October orchid is not as tardy as it may seem. Like
all living things, it stretches out toward the future even as
it fixes its roots in the past.

The stately elm bursts its buds in April while some of
its cousins, the nettles, withhold their peppery foliage
until July. Yet July is "spring" to the nettle just as April is

to the elm. And, despite our folklore, the pudgy wood-chuck, or groundhog, may enjoy spring long before his official Day, February 2—and long after it, too, whether he sees his shadow or not.

What mechanism runs this complicated clock that ticks on and on, picking up a new life here and dropping another there? How does it all fit in place? Who wakes the groundhog, anyway?

The answer gleams in a million beady eyes, peering out of grass clumps and hollow trees. It cries in the desperate battle of a sparrow against a nest robber forty times her size. It murmurs in the strange quietude of a swift-winged woodcock who sits the nest even while it is brought inside to be photographed. It whispers in the greening of a maple as the tree welcomes the summer—and sets embryonic buds against the distant winter. It shimmers in the insect-laden skies of an Indian summer against the afternoon sun.

Indeed, part of the answer as to the workings of this clock lies in the sun itself.

1

First Call

THE chickadee crouched motionless. Not a sound or move did he make; he might have been the statue of a bird. Although my face was only two feet from him, he gave no indication that he saw me. Ready to fly, he looked out over the snow and ice of the Vermont landscape.

Chickadees come and go all day at the windowsill feeder near my typewriter. There is seldom a time when there aren't several scrapping and sorting through the sunflower seeds. Sometimes there are as many as ten of them. Their activity generally accompanies the clatter of my rickety Underwood No. 5. Now it was the sudden stillness outside my window that caused me to turn and watch.

I looked toward the sugar maple. Another chickadee was perched upright on a branch, also unmoving. A white-breasted nuthatch clung to the underside of a limb, as if molded in clay.

Something, some peril, hung over my yardful of birds.

Snatching the binoculars, I raced downstairs and stole out on the steps for a better view.

Two blue jays sat in the wild cherry tree. A third sat some distance away, on the highest twig of our tall tamarack. Nothing seemed amiss; no great hawk circled or rested among the bare February branches. No cat lurked, half hidden, at the base of a bush. Yet not a bird moved. Now I could hear the warning whisper of the chickadees as it ran urgently through the trees: s-s-s-p! s-s-s-p! s-s-s-p!

The trouble had to be somewhere. While I considered the possibilities, my eye wandered back to that solitary jay in the tamarack. The bird wagged its tail. Just once.

In that instant, I understood. Jays don't move their tails like that. The binoculars quickly confirmed my hunch: this was no jay. It was the bird whose sudden appearance in a lone tree can "freeze" a hundred birds at once. It was the northern shrike, the bird whose very name tells, somehow, all about him.

At least that's how the name affects me. Rhyming with "strike," it connotes, swiftness, accuracy, singleness of purpose. Technically the shrike is a songbird, with a deceptively sweet warbling call. It feeds on insects as do many other songbirds. It seeks other prey, as well: small snakes, shrews and mice, and even its feathered neighbors. Swift of wing, the robin-sized marauder overtakes them in the air and batters them to earth. Then, true to its other name—butcherbird—it hangs them up on a thorn or piece of barbed wire the way meat is hung on hooks in a butcher shop.

Through the binoculars I could make out this key figure in my front-yard tableau. Pearly gray he was, with black wings and tail. He was white underneath, with a dark mask and a strong, black hooked beak. He lazily turned his head this way and that, surveying the motionless world below him. And all the while the chickadees watched him and warned each other.

Something caught his attention near our lilac bush. Drifting to the bush, he skilfully descended to its center. Now I could guess his next move. A maple limb hung low near the bush; crouched on one of the maple twigs was a tree sparrow. From the vantage point of the bush, the shrike could launch itself in a way that gave the sparrow no choice but to fly out into the open air.

And this is just what happened. Springing up, the butcherbird rose toward its chosen prey. Out over the river beyond our yard went the sparrow, with the powerful wings of the shrike beating the air behind it. As I watched, the two birds darted over the snow of our valley toward the trees and brush at the far edge of the meadow. The sparrow twisted and turned, but the shrike dogged its every move.

In a moment the gap between them was so small that I could see only the shrike. The only way I knew that the tree sparrow still lived was by the astonishing aerobatics of the larger bird. The shrike's wings, showing their white patches, flashed black against the snow. Finally the chase was lost to view among the birches and alders.

With the disappearance of the shrike, the smaller birds relaxed. The chickadee flew away from the feeder. The nuthatch continued its inspection of the maple limb. And my front yard reverted from a brief spring back into winter. For to us, in northern Vermont, the butcherbird is a harbinger of the season to come.

The shrike is a whole month ahead of the first robin and six weeks ahead of the bluebirds. While the snow is deep and the first crocus still buried in the earth, he begins a slow leisurely trek north from the middle states to his breeding grounds in New England and Canada. All along his route, doubtless, he meets the same nervous stillness that heralded his appearance in our tamarack. Even the shrike, early as he may be, is a come-lately among living things. He paused in our front yard on February ninth—only a week after we'd dutifully squinted at the sky on Groundhog Day. But Groundhog Day is not the start of things, either. The groundhog—or woodchuck, if you prefer—is hardly the alarm clock he's made out to be. Spring has infiltrated from a thousand directions before his first yawn.

The quickening of the pulse of life—in the groundhog's veins as in those of his neighbors—is regulated by the wanderings of our planet in its annual orbit. Tilted as it is on its axis, the earth presents first its upper and then its lower half to the direct rays of the sun in the course of a yearly tour.

You can see how this shift takes place by having someone walk around you with an ordinary school globe. Have him keep the axis of the globe pointed in a fixed direction—say, toward the door. You, the sun, stand in the center of the room.

Now have your friend give the globe a spin. Each revolution represents a twenty-four hour day. You'll note that the half of the globe tilted toward you gets your "rays" almost directly for a large part of every revolution—the long days of summer. The other half, slanted away, is in the shadow much of the time: winter's short days and long nights. As your friend goes half way around the room—half a year's circuit through the earth's orbit—the seasons on the two halves of the earth become reversed.

Magnify it all and you have the tilted earth swinging through space. It hurtles along in its half-billion-mile annual orbit, causing the days to shorten or lengthen and the seasons to change as it goes. So enormous is this cir-

cuit around our parent star that successive days vary by
only two minutes in a twenty-four hour period: one minute in the morning and one at night. Yet these minutes
are among the most important in all of life. Their steady
advance or decline affects the growing, the flowering, the
courtship and mating of our planet's living things.

Take those birds at my feeder, for example. Scarcely
have the days begun to lengthen after the low point of
December 21 than the chickadees start tuning up for the
season ahead. Each chickadee, instead of repeating his
own name in a chummy voice, breaks out into his spring
song. It doesn't matter if it is only a week after New
Year's and the tree trunks pop with the cold. A change is
in the air. When first you hear those notes, you'll find it
hard to believe that so sweet a whistle could come from
such a chatterbox.

It's easy to imitate the chickadee's "spring soon" call.
Whistle as high a note as you can for half a second. Then
drop down a tone and whistle another. The two notes,
that's all. The chances are a chickadee will answer you—
and follow his answer up with a close tour of inspection.
Sometimes you can start a yardful of them going. They
may even pass the call on to the neighboring woods.

Other birds declare the coming year. Watch the common English sparrow. As January becomes February he
dry-cleans his wardrobe for spring. At the tip of each
feather is a bit of grayish fuzz. This gives the English
sparrow a subdued tone, as if he'd been rolling in ashes.
Undoubtedly the fuzz helps to keep him warm. As the
weeks pass, the fuzz wears off, revealing the true colors of
the natty little cock-of-the-walk: black, white, tan, and a
rich chocolate brown. And so, without migrating or
changing a single feather, he keeps pace with the season.

The starlings in the park have yellower bills in late

February than they had at the start of the month. Their speckled plumage is glossier, too, with bolder spots. The pigeons flap their wings more loudly as they leap upward. And, if you're driving, you'll note more pigeons flying under highway bridges in February than in December and January. Breeding season is months away, but some vague stirring prompts them to explore the concrete abutments where they'll be nesting in May.

Notice the crows, too. Suddenly you begin to see them again. Perhaps they are back from a sheltered valley or the shore of a large body of water where temperatures fluctuate less wildly than in the hills. They've been scarce in upland regions during the bitter months. Now you discover them along roadsides and near villages as they feed on the remains of animals killed by automobiles. Their increasing frequency along the road points to a number of little tragedies.

Perhaps a skunk awoke from its fitful winter sleep to poke about at the edge of the highway, following the scent of a bit of sandwich or a candy wrapper. As it puttered along, its tiny stomach clamoring for food and its wakening senses yearning for companionship of its kind, it paid no heed to traffic. Or the victim might be a fox, yap-yap-yapping through the moonlight. Exhilarated by the nearness of the breeding season, the fox may have relaxed its caution for a fatal moment and ignored an oncoming set of headlights.

In the morning the sacrifices lie there by the snowy roadside, awaiting the crows. We in our automobiles speed down the highway, scarcely realizing what these scavenging birds are telling us of the coming spring.

Although for the crows there will be many weeks before the nesting season begins, there are a few birds that jump the gun completely. While we shiver and squint despairingly at the thermometer, the owls are abroad on business of their own. I hear them at night, calling to each other across my valley. Orion, the winter constellation, glitters above while the owls meet and mate and begin their families. So slowly do owls mature that they need a head start in life. Otherwise, the youngsters will not become self-sufficient by the following autumn.

If you're lucky, you may spot a female great horned owl in an old crow's nest or in the top of a broken stump. Sometimes the snow of the night before is still on her back. The owlets, dressed in heavy suits of thick down, are alert and ready to defend themselves with beak and claws from the time they're a few days of age. Spring has already come to them although your calendar is scarcely two months old.

This is an ideal time for a raptorial bird to raise her young, provided the family can stand the cold. There are no tree leaves to interfere with vision. Animals befuddled with sleep, feeling the pangs of hunger or driven by the first stirrings of the mating urge, throw caution aside. The result is a situation just made for a predator. So the owl drops right into place, as it were. She descends noiselessly toward a pair of frolicking cottontail rabbits—and bears one of the revellers away to her hungry offspring.

The mating urge soon begins to affect other birds. We like to watch the courtship displays of the nuthatches at our feeders. Normally these gray-black-white birds look alike, male and female. They act alike, too, up to some time in late January—selecting a sunflower seed and vaulting swiftly to a tree limb with it. There they poke their prize into a crack in the bark, using the tree as an anvil while they whack the seed open.

Then, one day, the nuthatches apparently make a momentous discovery: there *is* a difference between them.

When a female flies near a male, she is treated to an elaborate curtsy, complete with spread tail and expanded wings. The male follows up this display by selecting a sunflower seed and chasing her around the tree with it. At this time the female may not be particularly receptive and generally keeps out of his way. But as January drags through February into March the courtship is stepped up. The female happens to fly near the feeder almost every time the male is in evidence. He obligingly puts on his act. And now, when he pursues her with that sunflower seed, she's not quite so elusive. She may even condescend to accept the offering—although she's been choosing her own food all winter.

She may even go so far as to invite attention. I recall one female that greeted every male with a flutter of wings and a little nasal cry, like a fledgling begging to be fed. At first the males good-naturedly played the game and deposited seeds in her waiting beak. She must have been nothing but a tease, however, for they soon tried to ignore her.

Each male worked out his own answer to the problem. Two of them would hastily snatch a seed and escape with it to the old maple tree. One simply stayed away whenever the female appeared. It remained for the fourth male to put an end to the game. When he landed on the feeder, he was met with the shivering wings and baby talk. But he was equal to the occasion. Elaborately selecting from among the seeds on the tray, he hopped over to her and made his presentation: an empty husk.

She made another try or two at this male without success. Apparently she finally got the message, for she picked up a seed herself and flew away to the tree. There she became just another nuthatch again.

Not all birds go through antics as animated as those of

the "tip-up." This is what my neighbors call the nuthatch because of its habit of clinging to a tree head downwards. But even an everyday barnyard fowl has courtship behavior of some sort at this time. The turkey struts; the rooster flaps and crows; the cock sparrow drags his wings in the dirt and picks fights with other cock sparrows. In the woods the ruffed grouse thumps its wings in an increasing flurry of downbeats as it stands on a fallen log.

Such performances can happen any time, now that the days are getting longer. They're more than mere show: they're a vital prelude to the orderly process of courtship-mating-nesting. With each creature needing elbow room to raise its young, the drumming and strutting and crowing and fighting serve to establish an adequate territory.

February's brighter outlook can be noted in at least one very practical way. A friend of mine raises chickens. His flock supplies a number of our neighbors with eggs. "The low point of the season is late December and early January," he told me. "The hens don't produce many eggs then. If I can only get through January, I usually have enough eggs to supply my customers all summer."

His chickens, in a dollar-and-cents way, are bearing witness to the shift of the seasons. Indeed, so vital are those extra minutes of light per day that poultry raisers often supply illumination in increasing amounts in winter. This artificial daylight sends those reproductive hormones through the blood in greater quantity. And you and I eventually note the change in lowered prices as eggs become more plentiful.

Domestic chickens and turkeys and ducks are actually descendents of wilderness ancestors. Those steadily lengthening days affect their country cousins, too. If a pair of wild ducks can keep a patch of water open, they may stay around all winter instead of heading south. Then as early as February their own special New Year begins.

The males puff up their feathers and throw their heads back nearly to the tail. They chase each other and stand up so straight in the water they sometimes fall backwards. The females pay no attention to such foolishness. In fact, in the years that I've watched the antics of the males, I could swear the females go out of their way to ignore them. They wait until the males are at the height of their display—and at that moment the females stick their heads down into the mud. The drake has little choice but to present his grand finale to the unappreciative nether end of a duck tipped up in the water.

Eventually he gets his point across, however. In spite of the boredom with which she greets his efforts, the female allows herself to be persuaded. Sometimes she, too, may rush the season. Once I was poking through a Connecticut swamp in late February, trying to determine if the frogs had begun to lay their eggs yet. There were great pockets and patches of snow where winter still held its grip. Suddenly, from the base of a maple, a black duck burst into the air. It went careening over the swamp, while behind it a double handful of downy feathers settled back onto five white eggs.

The duck had pulled the feathers from her breast when she made her nest. Then she'd scattered them over her back and sides. Thus they'd slide off as she rose to fly away. The fluffy coverlet would provide concealment and insulation. The eggs would stay warm when she left to feed, even if they were laid more than a month ahead of time.

The nest—and the duck flying in a wide circle above

me—were the most obvious signs that spring was on the way. But, in reality, the whole swamp showed the advance of the season. If you have the chance to visit a swamp—or just a patch of woods—you can see for yourself.

The black-on-white of December has softened by February. The poplars, ashy-gray at the start of winter, show a hopeful tinge of green. A maple swamp somehow appears redder even though you can see only bare twigs and snow and dead grass. You never noticed how yellow the branches of a weeping willow were, either, or how shiny the bark of a cherry. And where did that red osier come from? This shrubby little dogwood of waste places has been growing there all along. Now its blood-red bark almost leaps out at you. Indeed, its bare branches have been called "the veins of spring."

If we could look beneath the somber bark of trees and bushes, we'd see the sap rising with the thermometer. That daily flow stirs the buds in their winter coating. It inflates them, as it were, bit by bit.

A bud that resembled a slender pine cone under the magnifying glass in December may look like a tiny pineapple in February. Our common shadbush, or serviceberry—often sold in nurseries as the Sarvis tree—has small pointed buds after its leaves have fallen. By March they may be twice their original size and look almost like stubby thorns poking out of the twig. The smoky color of the tree's bark brightens, as well—to a gray and black stripe fit for an ambassador's trousers.

Around the end of February the catkins of the swamp alders begin to loosen. They stretch a bit with each surge of the thermometer until they hang like the curls of a little girl. Then you push right through them, getting dusted with their yellow pollen as you look for the first spring flowers. Seldom does it occur that these are spring flowers, too.

Biggest and boldest in these late-winter woods is the plant with the marvelously descriptive name: the skunk cabbage. As it lies buried in the moist ground along a stream, the starchy root of this cousin of the calla lily responds to some hidden call. Scientists are still puzzled as to just how it goes about its annual rebirth, but undoubtedly it is affected by the sun it cannot see.

At any rate, often as early as January, enzymes in the root begin to change its starch to sugar. More of the sweet compound is produced than the plant needs, and the excess is converted into energy. This energy turns to heat, and the root warms itself. Now, with a cozy growing temperature two feet beneath the snow, the bud of the skunk cabbage begins to grow.

Up and up it presses, feeding and warming itself in a perfect bootstrap operation. So efficient is its little heat pocket that the plant may build up temperatures approaching that of the human body. And finally, one late-winter day, it gains the surface.

Often the snow has melted above it. The tiny underground furnace has warmed the earth, and the hooded flower finds itself in the midst of a circle of bare ground. The skunk cabbage is ready to be pollinated by insects, just as many of its still-slumbering cousins will be. But what insects are abroad on a February day?

A good part of the answer, if you wished to look for it, could be the cluster flies. In the attics of countless homes, these restless insects buzz against the windows and struggle to make their way outside. They have been slumbering since autumn, having entered houses through countless openings—the gaps between clapboards, spaces up under the roof, and around the edges of doors. Now they buzz to get out again. Those that elude the broom of the indignant housewife push through the cracks to the outside.

The flies careen off over the snow. Their dark bodies absorb the sun's heat and the activity of their tiny muscles keeps them warm. They join other insects abroad on this balmy day: crane flies, drone flies, caddis flies, gnats and midges. Their lives, too, may be linked to the existence of that portly plant with the skunky odor as it pokes up through the snow.

The peculiar aroma of the skunk cabbage is a bit like decaying meat—an illusion heightened by the purple-red streaks in the pointed elf-hood sheltering the little flowers within. Insects of many kinds, apparently intrigued by the sight and smell, clamber over the cloistered spadix of tiny yellow blossoms. They find a bit of nectar at each bloom. In the process they dust themselves liberally with pollen. Then they blunder around beneath the next hood, transferring the pollen to the waiting flowers. Thus the plant that gets up early, as it were, is fertilized by insects that cannot sleep either.

Nature, always canny, has even provided a built-in margin of safety for many of these early-rising blossoms. Skunk cabbage is large and smelly and conspicuous—apparently more so than it needs to be. It seldom lacks for a generous complement of visitors, but if insects fail to visit the more modest blooms of pussy willow or alder or birch, all is not lost. The lengthening male catkins shake in the breeze, scattering pollen on their ripening female counterparts. Self-fertilization, apparently, will do for now; better luck next year.

Even that off-season dandelion, venturing up through the snow, is equal to the occasion. Each of its hundred or

more female pistils comes up through a circle of male stamens. The pistil splits in two like the letter "Y," exposing
its fertile inner core beneath the protective outer tissue. If
no insects brave the chill winds, the two branches of the
"Y" split wider, curling downward upon themselves like
ram's horns.

Finally the receptive surface circles around until it
comes in contact with the pollen of the stamens at the
base of the pistil. Thus, in a pinch, the dandelion fertilizes
itself.

Not all the early insects are concerned with pollinating
the first flowers. Tiny gray springtails, so common at this
time that they're known as snow fleas, vault over the
snow. These animated yo-yos dance around by means of
a forked appendage that curves forward under the abdomen like the tail of a lobster. Spring-loaded, this appendage is cocked behind a trigger as you would cock your
finger behind your thumb to snap an object off a table.
When the trigger is released, the snow flea is catapulted
into the air.

The springtails hop about, an inch at a time, their gray
color absorbing warmth from the rays of the sun. With
the moderating temperature they resume their role, suspended during the coldest weather, of feeding on algae
and debris and old leaves—thus putting valuable food
substances back in circulation. As they leap around they
meet others of their kind among the snow crystals, and
make quick alliances that will soon produce pepper-grain
copies of themselves.

If you come tramping through the snow, each of your
footprints is a pitfall for the snow fleas; they tumble in
but cannot get out. In an hour or two your trail shows up
gray against white, with each track holding hundreds of
tiny prisoners.

The confinement turns out to be only temporary. As the shadows lengthen, the snow fleas begin to shun the light that called them forth in the first place. Now they burrow down to earth through the snow, thus escaping from your print.

Wander along a stream and you may find the remarkable winter stone fly. One of several related species, it has spent a year as a nymph beneath the stones of the stream, feeding on algae and other aquatic life. While countless living things are still imprisoned by the cold, the nymph crawls out of the icy water. Splitting its juvenile skin, it emerges as an adult, complete with two pairs of transparent wings and six sprawling legs.

Its dark-colored body warmed by the sun, the stone fly moves off across the snow. This insect does not feed when fully grown. Indeed, it probably cannot eat, for its mouth parts are feeble and reduced in size. It lives on borrowed time, as it were, subsisting on food stored in its body during the days of its adolescence. It can ration these reserves for perhaps a week of activity. Thus its brief adult life is all or nothing. If it meets another of the same species, the two may mate immediately. If not, the opportunity to reproduce itself will pass.

After her eggs have been fertilized, the female stone fly crawls back to the water. She drops her eggs in the stream with what remaining energy she has left. Then, dying, she lapses into immobility even as those eggs are hatching. The active little nymphs quickly seek shelter in the icy water. Thus a whole crop of winter stone flies passes the torch to a new generation almost at our feet while we search hopefully for signs of springtime.

On a late-winter day you may be surprised to find another hardy creature. Sailing out across the snow from the edge of the woods comes a brown and purple butterfly—one of the insects you'd least expect in February. This is the Mourning Cloak, or Camberwell Beauty, as it's known in Great Britain. Having slumbered in a hollow tree all winter, it now spreads its wings for a few short hours in the sun.

There may not be a single flower in sight, but the barren land still provides nourishment. Flying to a broken twig, the butterfly uncoils its long drinking tube. Probing around, it sponges the sweet sap oozing from the wound. Or, in these days of trash and litter, the mourning cloak sips a drop from the neck of a soft drink bottle by the wayside. Then it drifts back to the woodland, leaving you wondering if you really saw it at all.

If the day is warm enough you may see other butterflies, and perhaps a moth or two. The spunky little spring azure, scarcely larger than your thumbnail, quickly breaks out of its pupal shell and goes exploring on a warm afternoon. Cabbage butterflies flutter across the meadow like snowflakes gone astray. They are the vanguard of the millions of their kind that will dance over fields of radish and cabbage and broccoli later in the season.

The three or four successive summer broods of cabbage butterflies will be pale yellow with black wing tips. These early pioneers, however, are near-white. Perhaps their lighter color serves to camouflage them from birds as the butterflies skip over one snow patch after another.

Like the mourning cloak, the cabbage butterfly hunts for the delicate sweets of early spring. But even in the airy world of the butterfly, there's serious work to be done. I watched a cabbage butterfly one early March day along a New Hampshire road. The sun had melted much of the snow, and areas of bare ground made a patchwork of the countryside. The butterfly skipped along in seeming abandon, dipping down here and there for a moment and then lightly flitting away.

As I gazed at the scene, I realized the ground wasn't as bare as I'd thought. Every time the butterfly dropped to earth it touched the tip of its abdomen to a dark green rosette of leaves. On each new rosette it left a tiny white egg. The plants were winter cress, kale, and wild mustard —first cousins of the cabbage and turnips and cauliflower. These weeds would serve as platforms from which the new butterfly generation could be launched.

Then there are the "sap millers," as my Vermont neighbors call them. Small and inconspicuous, these moths can be found in almost any woodland. In Vermont they seek out the fluid that gives them their name. If you inspect one common species with dark markings on a light background, you'll discover every individual to be a male. The females are wingless, with velvety soft bodies and spindly legs. During those first warmer days they break out of their fragile cocoons in the humus near the tree bases. As they emerge they release a perfume that is detected by the feathery antennae of the males.

After the males have fertilized their flightless mates, the females make their way up the trunks of the trees. The same warm sun that called them forth has also swelled the buds just enough for the task at hand. Forcing the tip of her abdomen among the bud scales, each female deposits a few eggs. Then she dies, often still spread-eagled on the bark, where you discover her much later.

Incubating on those buds that will soon bring forth their new leaves, the eggs develop slowly as the weather abates. Then they hatch into those zany creatures fated to be gymnasts all their larval lives—the loopers or inchworms. I particularly like their scientific name, for it perfectly describes their stretch-hump-stretch-hump mode of progression: *Geometridae,* the earth measurers.

When I was a boy it seemed odd that some creatures would make their appearance in January and February instead of waiting for a more sensible time—April, say, or May. I wondered what rallying cry brought hundreds of "snow worms," as we called them, to walk on the surface of a drift as if mesmerized. Now I know that nature affords millions of little ecological niches—in time as well as space—each occupied by its own living things.

The snow worms, it turned out, are really several species of caterpillars. Awakened on a mild day, they promenade out over the broad, uncluttered boulevard of snow. They are preparing for spring, leaving the buried grass clump where they hatched and chewed and spent the winter.

By thinning their ranks, there is less risk that a wintering cluster of them will be gulped down by a bird, a shrew, or some other enemy. Besides, the flat surface of the snow makes for easy walking. Thus they can wander to potential new feeding places without having to clamber over twigs and grass to get there.

As a boy I was intrigued, too, by the wispy clouds of gnats that played up and down over the patches of open water in our brook. Now I know they had an appointment to keep. The mildness of a February day had called them to mate and lay their eggs. They would thus have come and gone before the more aggressive insects took their places, and before the swallows and flycatchers could arrive to reduce their active little congregations.

Often as children we would lie on the clear ice of our Connecticut brook and watch the slow-moving life below. We loved to see the aquatic insects, an occasional leech, and the drowsy minnows a few inches beneath our noses, awaiting the distant spring.

Every year the wood turtles in that brook would have a premating convocation. There were six or eight pools where they gathered in apparently aimless, uncommunicative assembly, three or four to a pool. They weren't there when I looked for them during Christmas vacation, yet by Valentine's Day they would have appeared. When the ice became opaque and spongy in early March, I would lose track of them, but with the spring thaw I could see them down there in the swirling water. They'd be paired by now, with the male perched on top of the shell of the female, peering down at her with a comic intensity.

By February other reptiles commence their family planning. A number of snakes may have started on a new generation. Called forth by some slight temperature change, or perhaps evicted by meltwater pouring into their dormitory, the snakes make their way into the sunlight. They come to the mouth of the old animal den where they've wintered in a closely packed mass, once described by John Burroughs as "a many-headed ball." They poke out from under a shelving ledge. They sprawl on stone walls for a few minutes of warmth, or slide through the boards of an old pile of lumber.

Lacking any limbs with which to caress his mate, the male snake provides an acceptable substitute by stroking her with his chin. I have seen a male blacksnake thus wooing his intended on the hood of an old junked car. They'd both made their way up from the shelter of its rusted-out interior for an early March sunning. And an abandoned stone-lined well at my Connecticut home would usually produce two or three pairs of intertwined garter snakes in late winter.

While snakes may mate as soon as they can crawl, many fish and frogs must wait until ice has left the shoreline in their ponds. Most of their egg laying takes place in the shallows. But "ice-out," as it is called, doesn't necessarily wait for the calendar. Living as I do along the banks of our little river, with several lakes and ponds nearby, I have discovered that this sign of winter's failing grip may come as early as January. Hard-bitten Vermonters, even as they watch the great floes plunge downstream, remind each other that the ice has to go out three times before spring is here for keeps.

Nevertheless, the first thaw is a crack in winter's shell. Indeed, for some creatures, the thaw becomes the start of their new season. To understand how this fresh hold on life is obtained, it may help to consider more closely this dramatic shift in a stream from winter to spring.

Ice-out on our river generally follows a period of calm, when the strengthening sun of the new year combines with a southerly breeze. The snow turns crystalline and granular—"corn snow," the skiers call it.

The drifts piled up along our road by the snowplow decay to a honeycomb texture. They freeze at night, but are so fragile that a touch sends a cascade of ice tinkling like breaking glass. In the daytime, snow and ice slump and crumble. Sometimes a patch of snow as large as a tennis court settles with a great sigh on our meadow as a few key granules finally give way.

Meltwater flows along beneath the snow. You can hear it whisper as you stand on a hillside. It forms tiny streams that join and flow along the edge of a rock here, a fallen log there, until they make their way to the brook.

The brooks carry their burdens to the river. The heavy river ice, anchored as it is to the rocks and shore, is at first unaffected by this spring-out-of-season. It stays in place while the water flows out from around its edges or spills onto it from the swollen brooks. The ice becomes a sort of false bottom—a foot-thick layer beneath the surface of the deepening water.

Suddenly a portion of the main ice gives way. Straining upward in its natural buoyancy, it tears from its anchorage. Sometimes it is frozen so tight to a rock that it lifts rock and all. Ponderously it rises to the surface—a sheet of ice weighing perhaps several tons. Then it begins to drift with the current.

Once under way, the ice has enormous power. It rides up on the ice immediately downstream, breaking it from its mooring. This ice, in turn, begins to shift. In less time than it takes to read this paragraph, several hundred feet of frozen river surface may be on the move.

That first release of pressure races downstream far faster than the flow of the water, in a swift chain reaction. One moment the river is calm, with that meltwater flowing over its icy surface. The next it is boiling, seething, thundering.

Individual floes rise like a surfacing whale, only to break in two and subside. Pieces of ice the size of an automobile slide up on the bank, pressing willows and alders to earth. Some temporary jam may cause the river to desert its old bed, carrying part of its cargo off into a field or even over a roadway. Then, when the water subsides, great chunks of ice may be stranded hundreds of feet from the river that brought them. There they stay, melting slowly in subsequent thaws, until May.

The river seldom stays at the flood. A spring thaw takes several days and now the warm spell is nearing its end. Occasionally a peal of thunder and a pelting rain help write the final chapter to the defeat of the ice. There'll be more cold weather, but winter's backbone has been broken.

Now, before the river freezes over again, some of the

aquatic life can gain a foothold on the season to come. Brook trout work their way upstream after such a thaw, headed for the smaller tributaries. There a few of them stay all spring and summer, spawning the following fall. Were they to try to enter the brook just before egg laying, they might be thwarted, as the tiny streams are often dry, except for a few pools, in late summer. Thus the first high water of the season helps set the stage for an event half a year away.

When the trout desert the large river for the smaller brooks, they place themselves in danger, for there is less room to maneuver. The mink follow close behind. I have watched mink exploring the edge of our pasture brook in their peculiar looping gait, slipping into each pool and investigating every rock where a trout might be hiding.

They catch many a fish, too, even those that seem perfectly safe. An honored country custom is to put a trout in the well or spring that furnishes your drinking supply. The trout keeps the well clean as it snaps up any insects that fall into the water. One February the trout in our rock-walled spring met its nemesis following a thaw. The spring filled to overflowing and ran down through our south meadow to the river. A mink, following the tiny freshet to its source, made quick work of our finny antipollution agent. We found him reduced to a couple of scraps on the bottom of the spring.

In addition to the fish and the mink, a few hopeful amphibians rouse themselves. A frog or two gropes its way out of the mud of the river bank and kicks around feebly at the edge of the water. Soon the ice will form again, but leopard frogs, pickerel frogs, and toads may come out for a few wakeful hours while the water flows free.

Their cousins, the spotted salamanders, sometimes waddle out from beneath their rotting logs and slip into the waters of a swamp or pool. There they will stay, scarcely moving, while ice thickens above them for perhaps a month more. But they are ready, like actors waiting for their cue. I have found spotted salamanders mating in a marshy spot at the base of our hillside while ice yet formed a roof over their watery chamber.

The water striders and whirligig beetles come out of hiding, too, for a few hours in the sun. The striders are those spraddle-legged bugs whose four largest feet distribute their weight on the water film so they can skate on the surface. They venture onto a chilly pool in search of insects that may have fallen into the stream. The shiny black whirligig beetles, looking like animated watermelon seeds, join in the scavenging.

The winter weather returns the next day. The movements of both insects become slow and deliberate. Soon they find their way back to the mud and roots at the edge of the stream. Their sleepy wanderings remind me of a man who wakes at night, stumbles to the icebox, and goes back to bed after a midnight snack.

Drowsy amphibians and water insects come in for their share of attention from predators, just as do the trout. They have to escape the raccoons that occasionally sozzle through the mud at the water's edge. Gifted with an exquisite sense of touch in those ten fingers, the raccoons feel through the icy muck and capture anything that wriggles. We often see their pawprints in the soft soil along the stream. The raccoons themselves, having taken the edge off a winter appetite that's finicky at best, have gone back to sleep.

Shrews, those smallest of mammals who live at such a frantic speed as to starve overnight if they have no food, constantly prowl the riverbanks. They swim out into the water after an escaping insect if necessary. The water shrew can even run on the surface, the long hairs on its twinkling feet keeping it from sinking.

Shrews burrow wherever the soil will yield to their efforts. Their appetites lead them to attack almost anything: insects, snails, centipedes, mice, and even other shrews. The spongy forest soil seldom freezes under its insulating blanket of snow, so the shrews make the floor of the woodland into a giant honeycomb as they seek all kinds of edibles.

With the advent of a thaw, there's a new food supply for these fierce little mammals. This is in the form of the earthworms that begin to work their way up to the surface from the lower layers of the soil. The shrews seek them eagerly, welcoming this change in their diet.

The bounty is not theirs alone, however. They must share it with the earthworms' constant companions, the moles. In autumn the moles follow their squirming prey down into the soil, to feed on them all winter below frost line. Then, as the worms slowly head for the surface in the waning weeks of winter, the moles rise with them. With their return, the householder finds mounds of fresh earth as the snow retreats from his lawns and meadows. The moles are back—a sign of spring that he'd rather not see.

You can note the approach of the new season in the actions of the animals in a city park or deserted lot. Squirrels spend hours in the treetops, chewing at buds that are swollen with the first new sap. Silhouetted against the sky the squirrels look like animated bird nests as they cling to the tips of the branches. You may hear a buck rabbit thumping the ground with his hind feet for the benefit of any interested females. On a smaller scale, the white-footed mouse drums on the earth with its front feet—a signal to mice of the opposite sex. It buzzes a similar message in a series of squeaks from its runway in the snow-matted grass.

Whether its a one-ounce mouse or a one-pound squirrel—or a one-ton block of river ice frozen in mid-thrust as it rides up over a jumble of its fellows in the now-refrozen stream, the message is the same:

February is done and gone. March has arrived at last. And whether it came in like a lion or a lamb, one thing is sure: already, in a host of bloodstreams and sap streams and woodland streams, spring is surging upward and outward. You can bet on it—just as sure as you can bet on sunrise tomorrow. One minute earlier than today.

2

"Wait for Me!"

ACROSS my meadow and five miles away on the eastern horizon is Mt. Abraham, four thousand feet high. As spring moves north, the warmth of the season floods up the slopes of the mountain like water rising in a container. We can note the progress of spring at a glance; each day the delicate green of bursting leaves is a little farther up the mountainside. According to scientists, spring climbs a mountain about a hundred feet a day and marches north approximately fifteen miles in the same period. Thus a person could hike from Florida to Maine in leisurely fashion and keep pace with the advancing front of the season.

If the hiker could watch over his shoulder, he'd see those tender buds gradually expand into full leaf, fifteen miles farther north each day. He would see flowers appear in regular procession, the time of bloom for any species also advancing at the same rate. He would watch insects flourish and die, each living its allotted span, laying

its eggs, and dropping to the ground. His northward progress would be like that of a boat through water, leaving
behind an expanding, changing wake of mammals, birds,
snails, trees, centipedes, and all their neighbors—each
acting its own part at the proper time in the pageant of
spring.

You and I, standing in one place, may get a different
perspective. We discover those early pussy willows and
snowbound robins shortly after spring's advancing front
has passed. Later we note the full bloom of the season.
Then, with the flood of it full upon us, we pick out the
last ripples of spring in the appearance of the latecomers.

At least they seem like latecomers to us. In reality the
time of their awakening is predetermined on their particular schedule; and if their schedule is upset, the results
could be fatal.

In the insect world, for instance, the praying mantis insulated her eggs the previous fall by depositing them in
an airy mass of bubbles. This mass hardened like buffy
styrofoam on a weed stem. All winter the frothy insulation protected the eggs, but it also guarded against too
hasty a response to the returning warmth. The mantis
young must not emerge too soon, for they require living,
moving prey. Hence they remain in their nursery until
there's an adequate supply of grasshopper nymphs, soft-
bodied aphids, and other new-hatched food in late spring.

Many predatory insects carry this built-in time lag. The
new generation waits until spring is established and the
table is spread. You seldom find the fierce nymphs of the
assassin bug until there are newborn caterpillars to assas-
sinate. Most tiger beetles remain in hiding until the
ground has warmed. Then there will be enough crawling
insects to feed them. The eggs of these swift-running warriors soon hatch into active, alert little grubs. The grubs

quickly burrow into the ground, there to lie in wait at the entrance to their burrows, lunging at any unwary insect that passes by.

Damselflies, those fluttery insects that look like small dragonflies but with wings held vertically instead of horizontally, lay their eggs in the tissues of water weeds. A fragile creature, the female damselfly must wait for the water to warm and the weeds to grow before the eggs can be laid. In many species, she descends completely beneath the surface for the task. Her mate holds her just behind the neck region by means of special claspers at the end of his long abdomen. He remains safely in the dry air while she goes below. Her duties finished, she signals the male, who hauls her back to the surface. The two fly away in tandem, searching for another spot to leave a few eggs on that May morning.

Those damselfly eggs, hidden as they are, might seem safe from harm in their subsurface incubator. However, no sooner are the eggs of many damselflies laid than a tiny wasp, *Polynema*, searches them out. Scarcely the size of a grain of rice, *Polynema* can "fly" beneath the water, using her paddle-shaped wings as oars.

When the little diver finds a damselfly egg she garnishes it with an egg of her own. Her miniature grub feeds on the tissues of the would-be damselfly nymph. This grub, in turn, may be preyed upon by still another wasp, *Tetrastichus*. Thus, when the damselfly egg finally produces a youngster, it may be any of three separate species.

Each link in this chain depends on the one before. And the chain stretches further than these three links. It reaches a year into the past, where hundreds of aquatic insect victims—each a part of its own chain—were consumed to bring those mating damselflies to maturity. The

chain stretches into the future, too, where the new-
hatched damselfly nymphs—or their parasites—serve as
food for other creatures. All these crisscrossing chains
thus become a complex tangle—often called by biologists
"the Web of Life." When one strand is plucked the whole
structure may vibrate.

While insect predators in this living web may have to
wait for their appointed time, their warm-blooded counterparts among the birds and mammals are less depen-
dent on the elements. For one thing, warm-blooded creatures carry their climate with them in their veins. In
addition, the diet of many birds and beasts of prey is less
restrictive than that of their insect neighbors. A fox can
eat last year's dried berries if rabbits are not yet abundant. It can even gain nourishment from a withered
mushroom. A screech owl can find a few insects or a frog
while waiting for the spring crop of mice. For this reason,
there are relatively few feathered and furred flesh eaters
in my woodlands listed among the late risers.

The migrant birds return from the south according to
the schedule of awakening life in the north. The first robins of spring—and the grackles and redwings and song
sparrows that appear at about the same time—can eke out
a living in the still-snowy landscape because they are so
adaptable. As long as they are well-fed, these early arrivals can withstand the last throes of winter. They take
any food they can get: last year's fruit still hanging on the
bushes, or the pill bugs and early spiders that venture out
for a sunning. The purple grackle systematically turns
over every old leaf on the ground, exposing lethargic
earthworms, dormant insects, and sluggish spiders.

Phoebes and other flycatchers arrive when the first insects begin to take flight. Beaks snapping, the flycatchers
dart out into the air near their chosen perches, thus earn-

ing their descriptive name. A bit later, when swarms of gnats begin to dance over the puddles and waterways, the swallows appear as if on a signal. These birds catch their food only on the wing. I've seen a half-dozen returning tree swallows descend from nowhere and slice their way back and forth through a thin veil of newly-fledged mosquitoes over a swamp. Life expectancy of one of these little insect pests may thus be less than a second, if a swallow nabs it just as it leaves the water. And on a good day our largest swallow, the purple martin, may catch ten thousand mosquitoes.

The main body of insects—the millions of aphids and caterpillars and beetle grubs—hatch just in time for the huge wave of migrating birds in May. These, the warblers and orioles and vireos, sweep through the trees in a singing, chattering swarm, cutting short a calamitous insect plague before it can get started. They are like the gulls that saved the Mormon pioneers from the locusts. Because this happens every spring, however, we scarcely realize the miracle that is taking place.

At last, when the plants are well in bloom, we can look for the arrival of that feathered jewel, the ruby-throated hummingbird. Its wings making a buzzing hum at up to two hundred beats per second, the tiny mote of life darts over the fields and gardens for the food it must have—the nectar of flowers.

So the timetable of the birds is related to their food. While scientists cannot say why birds migrate, they know that the ultimate success of the journey depends on whether there are adequate provisions when the birds arrive.

The spring parade of birds has its self-appointed master of ceremonies. Like a formal dinner party where each guest's arrival is proclaimed, the avian procession is heralded by an announcer of its own. This town crier—the common starling—shouting forth the birds that will follow as faithfully as if it had been employed for the job, is a bird of unusual talent. So perfect is its mimicry of whistles and chirps that it is tamed and kept for its imitative powers in various parts of the world.

The first starlings are among the earliest of birds. They appear at our Vermont farm in late February. There they sit in the treetops and go through a series of nondescript warblings and chatterings. Then, as clearly as if it had drifted down to us from its lofty circle in the sky, comes the scream of the redtailed hawk.

I look in vain, but no hawk is to be seen. Fixing my binoculars on the starlings, I discover what I suspect. It's that third starling from the left, say, who flutters his wings and opens that long yellow bill in a perfect hawk cry. It's a flawless performance, even though two or three weeks will pass before the first hawk is due to arrive on the scene.

A few days later, those early starlings depart for more northern lands. Their place is taken by new arrivals. And in a week I think I hear that first robin. It is only another starling, but my hopes are kindled, for the starling has announced that the robin is on the way.

Then, in mid-March, one member of the current wave of starlings makes my heart catch with its cry. From its raucous throat comes the liquid warble of that beloved harbinger of spring, the bluebird. And often, from the same starling flock, will come the flutelike notes of the "American nightingale"—the hermit thrush.

I have heard phoebes, song sparrows, redwing blackbirds, meadowlarks, and flickers announced by starlings. Almost always the glossy-feathered rowdies are about two weeks ahead of the birds they are imitating. It's as if the starlings had spent enough time with the bird in question to hear its song. Then the starlings, with their hardy constitutions and their pushy ways, go on ahead. As they travel, they repeat the songs of the birds they left behind. Each successive flock of starlings apparently has outdistanced the robins or the bluebirds or the flickers by a fortnight when it gets to my house. Here it replays the sounds of those slower-moving travelers like a many-voiced tape recorder.

When the real artist arrives, the starling yields to superior talent. It seldom imitates a bird that is actually on the scene. Now the other impersonators take over—the catbird, brown thrasher, and mockingbird. These mimics sprinkle the babble of their songs with phrases gleaned from their neighbors. But each spring the starling lends a note of expectancy to every new day as you wonder if that was really a killdeer you heard, say, or just his echo-in-advance.

The coming of the birds, like the activity of countless other lives, seeks to fill a niche in two worlds. First, there is the existence of the present, with its perils and the endless struggle for food. Then, too, there is the need to continue the species. Life in the wild may be cut short in a twinkling, as mosquitoes emerging from their pupal cases are snapped up by cruising swallows. Indeed, some male mosquitoes mate with the females before the latter have a chance to take flight, thereby gaining a few precious minutes of existence.

Thus the rising tide of birds, the flurry of awakening life, and the kaleidoscope of the flowering earth can be regarded as a bid today for a being tomorrow. That "being," of course, is through the offspring yet to be born, hatched, germinated.

In the insect world, countless eggs are swelling and releasing their tiny occupants. Often the first act of these hatchlings shows the marvelous economy of nature in preserving her vital commodities: the insects turn and eat the shell that imprisoned them. Thus they gain valuable nutrients while they remove the evidence of their existence from the scrutiny of enemies.

Adult insects resume the activities interrupted by the winter sleep. A lone crane fly stalks on spindly legs over a marshy spot in my south meadow. She touches the tip of her abdomen to the mud every few seconds. With each touch she deposits an egg. Out over the open water a dragonfly darts down as if stinging the surface. Every "sting" releases a tiny egg that drifts down to the bottom. Gnats and mosquitoes perform little ballets over rain puddles. They even bestow their progeny on the water in a tin can by the roadside.

Other insects, not yet mated, seek out the opposite members of their kind. Although some of their numbers go through courtship rituals—the sulfur butterflies, for instance, that chase the females straight up into the air like dry leaves caught in a whirlwind—much of insect mating is catch-as-catch-can. That flagrant annoyance, the housefly, merely turns his back on his winter hiding place and unites with the first female he can find. They fly around together for several minutes, the male piggyback on the female who feeds and walks and apparently doesn't realize he's there. Then they part company, going their separate ways until the next opportunity comes along.

Some beetles attach end-to-end so they face in opposite directions. In this position the female proceeds on her way while the male bumps along in reverse. If they come across some bit of food, the two of them may eat at separate tables, as it were, nonchalantly partaking of a meal while still coupled.

Honeybees have spring-cleaning to do. During the winter they kept alive by constant activity, gently fanning their wings and clustering together for warmth. Not all their number have survived the winter, however. Now the living must put things in order. The dead bees are dragged to the entrance of the hive and dumped out the front door. Old pieces of honeycomb are reprocessed by being chewed, or tossed aside with the rest of the debris.

There's another type of spring-cleaning in the hive. Although a single queen per colony is the rule, new queens are occasionally produced. Then one queen, with a few thousand worker bees, moves out to a less crowded home-site. The congregation that goes with her fills up on honey before leaving. The voyagers set forth as a dense swarm, usually to a spot previously selected by scouts.

The swarm is a reproductive process as well. If the hive is likened to a many-celled creature with each bee as one of the cells, its swarming resembles some sort of giant organism splitting in two. And, indeed, the likeness is impressive: a single worker out of contact with the hive soon perishes, like a tiny fragment cut away from a living body. In the togetherness of the swarm each bee can flourish just as all the cells prosper in a transplanted shoot.

Another swarm more widespread than that of the bees is largely responsible for that sport of purists—the art of dry fly fishing. Many fishing flies are an attempt to imitate insects stranded on the surface of the water. One of the most popular of these insects with trout—and with trout fishermen—is the mayfly. It gets its name from the month in which it appears on the scene.

There are more than a hundred species of mayfly in North America. Their nymphs, or naiads, feed on bits of algae. They creep about over stones and water weeds, or undulate gracefully through the water. Projecting out on either side are several pairs of feathery gills. After a period of months or years as a naiad the mayfly emerges into the air for one of the shortest adult lifespans of any living creature. Indeed, many mayflies that leave the water in the morning are dead by sundown.

Climbing out of the water, the naiad splits its skin. It carefully pulls itself out of its juvenile garments, leaving a perfect shell behind: still-clinging legs, delicate gills, and all. The new creature has gauzy, transparent wings. It may flutter around for a few minutes and molt again—the only type of insect to cast its skin after it can fly.

Now, even as it is fully adult, the mayfly is in the closing hours of its life. The time is so short that it has no need of a digestive tract. Indeed, its intestine has neither an entrance nor an exit; it's merely a tube filled with air that gives the feathery creature still more buoyancy.

Finding another member of its kind, the mayfly clings to it for a brief mating. Then, its delicate body already failing in strength, it flutters back to the stream. Here it rests on the water, its wings held upright over its back.

It is at this point in the life of the insect that the fish rise to the surface. With a good "hatch" of mayflies the water will be dimpled with feeding trout. And the fisherman, with his Royal Coachman and Silver Doctor and Parmacheenee Belle, endeavors to take his share. The fuzzy body of his dry fly, the double threads sticking out to the rear, and the tiny uplifted feather "wings" complete the illusion—at least in the eye of the man with the rod. Sometimes the fish is fooled, too. It takes a snap at the odd creation—and another trout is added to the creel.

A few hours after mating, the female mayfly extrudes the fertilized eggs like two streams of granulated toothpaste. Sometimes she dies before the eggs are released into the water. Her body becomes their incubator until they are freed when she is dashed to pieces in the current.

Thus ends the transient life of the insect honored each spring by millions of fishermen, although really known to just a few: the mayfly, whose scientific name, *Ephemerida*, means "living for only a day." That day, however, is sufficient for the continuation of the species. Fossils indicate that mayflies greeted the late-spring warmth along with the dinosaurs.

Many insects, on the quest for food or the companionship of others of their kind, may find their search temporarily halted by one of the tricks of the weather at this time of year: an April shower. To relatively large animals a shower is just a temporary inconvenience—if indeed they take any note of it. Deer and skunks and other sizable mammals wander around in all but the heaviest downpour, going about their lives with little change. Smaller mammals and birds are more sprightly than usual, darting about and frequently shaking off water in a little fountain of spray.

To an insect, however, a direct hit by a raindrop may be calamitous. Even a moderate fall of rain sends black flies and mosquitoes and other small flying insects to the shelter of the underside of a limb or an overhanging piece of bark. Crawling insects seek refuge under stones and debris, sometimes floating away half-drowned if the water floods them out.

At the same time there are a number of creatures to whom the spring rain is a call to action. Snails and slugs leave their winter hiding places beneath logs and stones.

They flow along over the wet surface of the earth, gliding on a film of mucus laid down by glands in the sole of the flat "foot" on which they travel. So viscous is that slippery pathway and so delicate is a snail's sense of touch that it can glide lengthwise of a razor's edge without harm. Thus it can travel over almost any ground when there is rain to keep it moist and lubricate its trail. The wet earth is to a snail or slug what the surface of the snow must be to those insects that travel on a sunny day in winter: a chance to wander in any direction and find a spot for a new home.

The best known traveler in this rainy-day world is the familiar earthworm, or nightcrawler. Exquisitely sensitive to vibrations in the soil, it easily detects the drumming of the raindrops and hurries to the surface. There, with the rain keeping its delicate skin moist, the earthworm stretches out from its burrow in search of food. Finding a shred of grass or an old leaf, the worm maneuvers it around with its prehensile lip and draws its prize down into the ground.

Should two earthworms happen to meet, their activities take on a new purpose. Earthworms are true hermaphrodites, each worm having complete male and female organs arranged in tandem at the anterior end. The two worms approach from opposite directions and lie side by side, with the genital openings of one worm opposite those of the other. A slime tube is formed, through which the two exchange sperm cells.

After this impromptu mating, the worms go their separate ways. Several days later the now-fertilized eggs of each are released into a fleshy collar near its anterior. The collar slides forward, puckers into a capsule as it is forced off the end of the worm, and a few dozen thread-like larvae will be born in a week or two.

Another creature of the rain is the red eft, a salamander about the length of your little finger. Hatched the year before, the eft began life as an aquatic larva. It grew slowly most of the summer, snapping up water insects, tiny crustaceans and other salamanders smaller than itself. Then, as fall approached, the eft crawled out on land, changed from olive green to brick red in color, and spent the winter in a rotting log or clump of leaves.

Any spring rain may bring it out again. The astonishing color of its body, ornamented with small vermilion spots, is apparently a warning device, for the red eft secretes a distasteful substance from glands of the skin. Probably the first of these salamanders to be attacked by a predator loses its life while its captor learns its lesson the hard way, but subsequent red efts are safe from attack. Hence they will travel in relative safety for another year, plodding along on rainy days until a third spring calls them back to the water to lay their eggs.

Each returnee becomes a pond salamander, or newt, and resumes its greenish appearance. Its belly takes on the color of egg yolk dotted with black pepper. Its taste must remain quite peppery, too, for I have often seen these four-inch amphibians swimming lazily a few inches from a northern pike or bass—neither paying any attention to the other.

Most vocal of the amphibians, the frogs put in an appearance on these April days. Wood frogs and spring peepers seem hardly able to wait: they may have been croaking and peeping respectively before most of the ice was off the ponds. Now the rest of the long-legged tribe —the leopard frogs, grass frogs, and toads—finally stir into action.

These goggle-eyed amphibians poke out from the debris of a rotting log. They burrow up through layers of leaf humus or kick themselves free of the mud of several months' hibernation. Then they make their way to the edge of a swamp or pond to assert themselves in croaks and grunts and squeaks.

The males are usually first to arrive. Each frog and toad has its distinctive sound. The frog inflates its throat or sides or neck, depending on the species. Thus it makes a resonance chamber for its croak, chirp, or bellow, as the case may be.

The females, apparently not gifted with enough subterfuge to be coy, leap tardily into the melee. There they evoke a round of thrashings and gurglings and croakings among their suitors. These worthies clasp every moving object, regardless of sex, in an embrace that will ultimately result in (1) the extrusion of hundreds of jelly-covered eggs if the frog grasped is a female, or (2) an outraged squawk and a monumental kicking if he is not.

Spring fever, if you can call it that, finds its belated way beyond the frogs to the creatures in the water around them. The walleye and carp breed in the shallows, as do many fish. Now that the ice has left the rivers and pond edges something happens to the walleyes. The female swims about in circles with one or more males of her kind. She may pause, trembling, in a moment of apparent anticipation. Then she is off like a torpedo.

Darting through the shallows along the shore, the walleye rolls and twists, strewing eggs right and left. Behind her comes the male, scattering milt with equal abandon. Other males may follow, their added milt serving as insurance that every egg will be fertilized. The chase may subside as quickly as it began, to be resumed the following day.

At last, when the female has disposed of as many as

fifty thousand eggs, she drifts away to the depths to re-sume life as a glassy-eyed, impassive fish.

The carp spawns in the backwaters of lakes and ponds. We frequently come across a carp convocation in the "slangs," or flooded river mouths leading into Lake Champlain, during our bird walks in April and May. To many sportsmen there are few fish lowlier than a carp; it does little more than muddy the water and come in at the end of a line like an old boot. But again the lengthening days of spring effect their transformation.

Working back into the shallowest water that will allow it to swim, the carp is joined by its fellows. There, with its back often rising above the surface, it races and wal-lows and chases its companions in the weeds until the water becomes liquid mud.

I've seen great carp weighing ten pounds or more ram themselves up on shore in a transport of piscine ecstasy. The females drop their eggs and the males strew their sperm. Doubtless they rely on the laws of chance for fer-tilization, as it must be impossible to determine the sex of one's neighbor—at least by sight or feel—in all that murk. But the thrashing tails and the swirling bodies blend male and female sex products together as thoroughly as an eggbeater.

Other fish give their salute to spring—the black bass and sunfish, for instance, that sweep a circle clear on the gravelly bottom in the shallows. There they protect their eggs against all comers, from minnows to muskrats. Yel-low perch drape their strings of eggs over weeds and sub-merged brush near the water's edge.

The bowfin creates a clearing in the jungle of water plants, from which radiate several pathways. Female bowfins, pausing as if by accident at the mouths of these paths, allow themselves to be enticed to the center. There each female contributes a few hundred eggs and goes her way. An enterprising male may thus be responsible for as many as fifty thousand youngsters, who hatch in ten days. These small fry soon strike out for deeper water, accompanied by their watchful father, who challenges other fish, canoes, and even startled swimmers on their behalf.

Fish, breeding clear into June, may seem slow to begin their family duties when compared to other creatures in the air and on the land. But water takes a while to warm up, so the chilly creatures are on a slower timetable. And fortunate they are to be slow, for the shallows where they might have laid their eggs earlier would be nothing but matted grass when spring's high water subsided.

Sometimes, in spite of this built-in biological "hold," a premature dry spell shrinks the pond too fast. Perch eggs become gluey ropes, drying helplessly above the retreating water, while the solicitous sunfish and bowfins must abandon their potential families for deeper water.

Parental care in fish is hardly a rarity. Fish fanciers know about mouth-breeders and bubble nesters and the male seahorse that carries his mate's developing eggs in a pouch. But care for the young in the insect world is far more unusual. With the exception of termites, ants, bees, and wasps there are few insects that ever live to see their young. The majority of insects die soon after the eggs are laid. Yet right in the shallows of a pond or sluggish stream can be found one of the rare exceptions to the general rule that most insects are orphans: *Belastoma*, the brown water bug.

These bugs hunt through the water, their grasping front legs hugging insects and tadpoles to them while they suck the victim's vital fluids with a pointed beak.

Most of the time these creatures are solitary. In spring, however, their antisocial ways are mellowed—at least, toward others of their kind. The male couples with his larger mate in the fashion of most insects. He clings to her with those raptorial forelegs as she goes about her business of getting a living. Sometimes when she catches a fish or tadpole, he plunges his own beak into the hapless creature, like an extra straw in the soda.

With mating completed, the female turns on her erstwhile suitor and seizes him in a vise-grip. Maneuvering his struggling body into position, she proceeds to decorate his back with her eggs. Each egg is glued in place with a cement that hardens on contact with water. Then she releases the male and swims away, freed of all maternal duties.

As the male bug basks at the surface, the warm May sun incubates the eggs. An earlier sun would be too feeble, while the direct summer sun might be too hot. He carries their brood until the nymphs hatch and seek their own fierce little fortunes.

Other insects cruise the waters. They climb on weeds or creep over the bottom, many of them absorbed in the business of replenishing the pond with more of their kind. Snails fasten little jellied capsules, a dozen eggs in each, on rocks and sunken sticks. Aquatic earthworms, leeches, flatworms meet and mate in the mud. For them, too, these warm May days are just right: neither too hot nor too cold.

Freshwater mussels expel clouds of tiny larvae, or "glochidia," from their brood cavities. Looking like lively grains of sand, the glochidia move through the water for short distances by convulsive snaps of their tiny, toothed shells. If the shell happens to clamp onto the fins or gills of a fish, the mussel holds tight. It rides about on its unwilling host, absorbing nourishment from the fish's body fluids.

Thus the mollusc, unable to do more than plow slowly through the mud as an adult, may be carried far from its birthplace. After a few weeks it has attained the size of a grain of rice. It drops from the fish and settles to the bottom of the pond. There it burrows part way into the mud and develops into the stolid, uninspiring mussel whose shell may be fated to become a few mother-of-pearl buttons.

The freshwater mussel's thick shell is no guarantee against some of its strong-jawed neighbors. The otter's two or three kits, born blind and helpless in a riverbank den in mid-April, soon clamor for more than their mother's milk. The female, swift enough to overtake a trout or salmon, sometimes seeks easier, if less easily chewed, prey in the form of those mussels. Hauling the molluscs to the surface, the female can often crack them with her powerful teeth. Sometimes she floats on her back, using her chest as a table in the manner of her rare cousin, the sea otter.

Raccoons have four or five youngsters to feed, too. They crush and eat the smaller mussels when they get the chance. Although a full-sized mussel may be too hard for a raccoon to crack, the black-masked little prowler seems to be an incurable optimist. I have come across a raccoon vainly trying to bite its way into a mussel about the size of a flattened lemon, if you can picture such an object. Every time the raccoon clamped down for a good bite, the smooth-shelled mussel would practically squirt out of its mouth.

Frustrated, the raccoon batted the mussel along the ground for a while. Then it dumped the obdurate mollusc into the water and washed it thoroughly, which helped not at all. Finally, outmaneuvered, the raccoon gave up and walked away.

The muskrat, however, has solved the enigma of the mussel. She uses the weapon denied to the active, inquisitive raccoon: patience. Spreading a supply of mussels out on dry land, the muskrat bides her time. Once or twice she may turn them over like a solicitous housewife spreading clothes to dry. The sun soon accomplishes what teeth and jaws might fail to do, and the shell gapes open. Then this webfooted cousin of the meadow mouse consumes the mussel and swims off to nurse her half dozen kits in their lodge of mud and reeds.

The muskrat often lives in ponds built by the beaver, North America's largest native rodent. Sometimes weighing more than fifty pounds, the beaver is also busy with domestic affairs on these early May mornings. Almost exclusively vegetarian, it makes its meal of the "bark, buds and twigs of tall trees," to quote an old natural history book on my shelves. The book neglected to elaborate as to how the beaver got its food, thus making it sound like a tree-climbing animal. Of course it actually cuts the trees and doesn't climb them at all.

The beaver has such an inordinate fondness for the shoots of poplar that my wife Peg and I amuse ourselves by tossing a few poplar branches into a local beaver pond at dusk on a May evening. Soon the female swims out from beneath her well-knit lodge of mud, sticks, and stones. She seizes a branch and floats at the surface, holding a twig by the fingers of a little black hand, while she chews on it like a child with a stick of candy.

After a moment she dives, carrying a piece of the poplar with her. We hear the mewing of the kits as they welcome their mother. Then the mewing falls silent, and all we hear from the lodge is the busy crunch, crunch as four or five sets of teeth make short work of this gift from that unknown outer world.

Occasionally the beaver's cousin, the woodchuck, departs from its landlubber ways and swims like its aquatic relative. A female 'chuck on our property had a den beneath a rockpile at the edge of the New Haven River. Once or twice a week I could spot her swimming across the river to forage on the clover and dandelions on the far side. By late May her four youngsters accompanied her, plunging in and coming out on the other bank as if woodchucks swam all the time.

Generally, however, these are creatures of meadows and overgrown brushland. There they dig burrows that may serve as dens for rabbits, skunks, foxes, and raccoons —or emergency escape holes for almost any animal in a fire, or when hard pressed by an enemy. Thus woodchucks are a valuable part of the landscape, often outweighing their damage to alfalfa and other crops.

This time of year the female 'chuck is apt to indulge in that age-old feminine pursuit of rearranging the furniture. She includes the youngsters in her activities, hauling them off to a new burrow almost anytime. I've seen a female with a baby wrapped around her chin like a collar while she held it gently by the belly skin with her teeth.

By moving about she accomplishes an unexpected result: she leaves a whole population of fleas and mites behind—stranding them until they can hitch a ride on some animal that happens to poke into the abandoned burrow. You may see the woodchuck version of spring-cleaning almost anywhere east of the Mississippi.

The woodchuck's cousins, the tree squirrels, move their youngsters around, too, sometimes toting the babies to as many as five different homes before spring fever finally subsides. Such a wanderlust helps account for all those leafy nests in the trees. They make it look as if the land were invaded by squirrels.

On a spring ride in the country you may find your vehicle bearing down on that legendary poke-along, the turtle. She, too, is on a domestic errand. Now that mating is a thing of the past she has to allow her eggs to ripen by depositing them in the sand. They need an entire summer to hatch, and she goes at her task as soon as air and earth are warm enough—and these spring days are long enough to set some mysterious inner machinery in motion. Deserting her pond or stream, she wanders right across the road, heedless of traffic.

To me it's heartrending to see one of these slow-moving reptiles caught in a stream of cars. I want to stop for her, but I'd precipitate a bumper-to-bumper chain reaction. And so I swerve a bit to straddle her, hoping the cars behind me will do the same. Then I reflect on a world that permits a turtle to exist through the days of the dinosaurs and a hundred million years thereafter— and yet snuffs her life out beneath the wheels invented by a two-legged creature who was born just yesterday.

Incidentally, if you do happen to rescue one of these unhurried creatures in the road, place her on the bank toward which she was heading. Don't return her to the original side. Turtles are strictly "one-way" until after those eggs have been laid. So, no matter where you place the female, she'll doggedly head for that unknown but beckoning spot across the road.

The animal world, of course, has no exclusive option on the need to reproduce its kind. The greening and growing and flowering of plants accelerates with the lengthening days. In many cases they have been waiting their turn as surely as their livelier animal neighbors.

Some weed seeds, for instance, have a chemical in their coating that inhibits germination. This chemical is slightly water-soluble, being washed off after receiving the proper amount of rainfall and melting snow. Then the seed is able to germinate. Other seeds, such as those of some grasses, have a long tail that coils and uncoils with varying moisture like a watch spring. The action of this tail, renewed with each rain, causes the slender seed to be driven into the soil like a drill. And with almost any seed, of course, sprouting takes place only when conditions of moisture and temperature are right.

Spring floods wash seeds into the ground where they are hidden—and thus planted—in the mud. Fungus galls, like the black knot of cherry and the cedar-apple rust, have remained dry and apparently lifeless all winter. Now they produce spores that can travel for miles on the wind or the feet of birds to the tender foliage of a new host. One fungus is built like a diminutive bird's nest the size of a raisin. Its "eggs" are four fragile pouches that contain thousands of spores. A dead-center hit by a single raindrop on a birdnest fungus creates a compression that causes the pouches to rupture instantaneously, sending their spores out with the splash of the same raindrop.

The flowers of April and May, seemingly appearing at random, also may have had to wait for the proper conditions. And those conditions—warmth and moisture and the increasing length of the days—become right for an estimated two dozen awakening species of wildflowers each week in my section of the northeast. Add to these the rebirth of hundreds of species of grasses and trees and mosses and you have some idea of the scope of this annual green explosion.

These spring flowers seem less pretentious in their colors than the riot of summer blossoms. A great many early blooms are plain white or yellow, with a few blues. There's a theory explaining the reason for this forthright coloration: these are high-visibility pigments, easily spotted by early bees and other pioneering insects.

Honeybees, it seems, are largely colorblind to the red end of the spectrum. Hence the whites and yellows of spring beauty and hepatica and anemone and cinquefoil —and the blues of early iris and flag and violets—may stand a good chance of the pollination needed in their struggle for life. Some pink flowers depend on the admixture of white in their colors for visibility, while others utilize sweet smells to attract insects. Later, when the world is alive with flies and beetles and butterflies, the flowers take on all the hues of the rainbow. Except for the cardinal flower, however, few wild blossoms are pure red.

Each flower and leaf adds its own color to the spring parade as it stirs into life. After the awakening hues of the twigs and branches follows the greening of the carpet of grass. Then comes the crazy quilt of spring flowers. From mid-April to May you'll see what look like puffs of steam among the trees: the shadblow or serviceberry is in bloom. Its mass of white flowers with their slender petals told the American Indians and early settlers the time had come for that delicious fish, the shad, to run up the rivers for spawning.

Today the shrubby tree still blooms at the appointed time, although its silvery namesake no longer swims most of our polluted waters. A few days later the dogwood bursts into bloom. You'll also see the delicate pea-green of the flowers of sassafras—another small tree which, like the shadblow, has been able to survive along modern roadsides.

Yellow carpets in swamps and wet meadows signify the marsh marigold or cowslip. We gather them each spring for a mess of greens while they're still in the bud. In mid-May delicate pinks and whites appear as fragrant wild cherries and plums bid for the attention of the bees. The procession of flowers continues until unappreciative highway crews come along with mowing machines and weed killers, and until the farmer cuts his first hay crop from the meadow.

Thus it goes in these days of preparation and fertility and new growth. Your very next step could place you in the midst of a dozen new lives. Perhaps you note that a new leaf on the end of a cherry twig is bumpy and curled. Straighten it out and you'll find its underside sprinkled with eight or ten aphids—plant lice whose span from one generation to the next may be only two weeks. In a month these ten will have turned to thousands.

A ladybird beetle climbs toward the aphids. This beetle is one of the few insects that even the most squeamish girl will usually allow to crawl on her hand. Yet, despite its attractive colors and roly-poly appearance, the "ladybug" is a tiger in its own small world. It is an inveterate foe of those soft-bodied aphids and their cousins, the mealy bugs and scale insects. Its larvae are voracious little grubs, clipping through the ranks of their thick-packed prey. Neither the plant-feeding aphids nor the aphid-eating ladybird larvae could have hatched earlier; the life cycle of both depends on tender young leaves.

A few ladybird beetles have, in effect, succeeded in shortcutting the progression of plant-to-aphid-to-ladybird. They gain their nourishment from the plants first hand, rather than getting it by eating the sap-drinking aphids or scale insects. One of the most notorious is the Mexican bean beetle, who attacks your garden beans shortly after they have sprouted. I love the bean beetle's scientific name: *Epilachna corrupta*—freely translated, "the unlady-like ladybird."

Look around you. Lift an old board. Pull apart a rotting log. You'll find ants under a sun-baked stone, warming the pupae of their younger sisters—mistakenly called "ant eggs"—beneath this natural radiator. Put your ear to a decaying stump and hear the crusty scratching of a long-horned beetle, fighting its way to the outside following a wood-borer childhood.

Smell the odor of fresh earth. Inhale the perfume of flowers. Drink in the sight of a spring hillside: the green of new grass, the brown of the old, the dots of color from ten thousand blossoms. Taste the wintergreen flavor of the sap in new yellow birch twigs, the bitter almond of young cherry bark.

These are a few of the sights and smells and sounds of the seeming slowpokes of April and May. It's been a struggle, but they made it.

Just in time to join the spring parade—even if they're rooted to the spot.

3

Summer Summons

ALL spring they followed that mountain highway. We could see one or more on almost any day we looked: the hawks returning from the south, riding the air currents along the ridge of Mount Abraham. Soaring in progressive circles or striking out in long, flat glides, each of them may be in the view of our binoculars for ten or fifteen minutes before it disappears in the direction of the Canadian border, seventy miles to the north.

Its place is shortly taken by another hawk or two, also steadily drifting northward. We have identified ten species of these large birds, plus the osprey and even two bald eagles. Then, sometime around the middle of May, comes a day when not all of the hawks continue on their way. One of them remains, circling higher with each wheeling turn. As it banks and affords a momentary glimpse of its upper surface, a hint of a rust-colored tail comes to our straining eyes.

She has returned. Our red-tailed hawk, latest member

of the aerial squadron that has been moving north for more than three months, has survived one more round trip to her wintering grounds. Now she takes the place she will occupy all summer and becomes our sentinel in the sky.

She is not the only one of her species to travel this ridge, nor even the last. We see migrating red-tails as early as February and as late as June. Each of them is on its own pilgrimage to some familiar spot where it has nested year after year. Our particular female has a bulky aerie of twigs and leaves on the top of a huge white birch, half a mile from Lincoln Gap. She has added to it each year until the scraggly platform is the size of a truck tire.

How do we know that this speck in the blue sky is a female? In truth, we don't—not at first. But we have seen her for six years now, and she often patrols the air within a quarter mile of the nest, north of Lincoln Gap. Her mate hunts south of the gap, or swings far around the nest in circles two miles wide. Then, too, our first view of this hawk, when she was closer to us, showed her immense size: body two feet long, with a wingspan of four feet. The male is somewhat smaller, lacking a few inches in both dimensions, although it is hard to compare sizes unless you see both birds.

A favorable shift in the wind confirms our hunch. Off to the south we hear the cry of the male. It is a wild, slow scream with a falling inflection, repeated once a second. We can catch but three such cries before the wind changes again. Although we peer so intently that tears come to our eyes, the second hawk is not to be seen. Then the puffy cumulus clouds shift position and there he is—circling among them, the merest fleck of dark against white.

It seems impossible that that scream, piercing as it is, could come down to us from a bird so far away. But that cry—and those lofty circles nearly a mile above the earth —are the hawk's way of declaring his domain. No alien red-tail had better miss these warnings. The male—or his mate, for that matter—would plummet down on half-closed wings to rake the intruder with those punishing talons.

Now that the red-tail and her mate were back, summer was under way. We would be able to find the hawks, seemingly suspended up there in the sky, for the entire season. They would be benevolent despots, exacting tribute in the form of chipmunks and mice and snakes, while keeping their prey strong and alert by weeding out the slower individuals.

Small birds have little to fear from these large soaring hawks and scarcely seem to notice the high flying predators. Let one of the smaller, swifter hawks appear, however, and the birds are on the alert. Although apparently not half-paralyzed as they are in the presence of a shrike, they go about their activities furtively, quickly, with an eye to that intruder half-hidden in a nearby tree. This feathered bandit—a Cooper's hawk, say, or a sharp-shin—also keeps his prey honed to a fine edge. He serves an important role in culling out the less wary or sickly birds.

Like the hawks, these smaller birds set up circles of territory when they return to their breeding grounds. Their boundaries are proclaimed by song. Those vocal efforts, melodious as they are, contain a warning to males of the same species: Keep away. These other males, in turn, issue similar proclamations from their own trees or bushes.

Shortly after the males have established their home

limits, the females arrive. Each female, on choosing a
mate, joins him in driving other members of the species
away. Thus a pair of birds will have enough space to provide food for a family. Our red-tail hawks, needing a rabbit or its equivalent in fresh meat daily, claim a whole
mountainside for their two youngsters. A pair of song
sparrows, on the other hand, able to eat almost anything,
can raise a brood in a corner of your garden.

Vocal claims to territory are backed up by fights along
disputed borders. It's common to see two robins running
side by side on a lawn, ostensibly looking for earthworms
but each really daring the other to step over that bound-
ary. And one of them usually does—until, after a series of
skirmishes, a battle line is drawn.

From then on an uneasy truce prevails, with each bird
reaffirming his claim daily at the top of his lungs. Birds of
different species may nest in a robin's kingdom: sparrows,
wrens, finches, vireos, to name a few—but except for his
mate, no other robins are allowed. And the other kinds of
birds establish similar circles of their own.

These musical "no trespassing" signs, though invisible,
are well-nigh unshakable. This was pointed out to me by
a friend who received a phonograph record of bird calls
for Christmas. She sat in her living room on those long
winter evenings, listening to the songs and matching
them with the pictures in her bird book. By spring she
was able to recognize the notes of many songsters before
she ever saw the birds themselves.

In May a Baltimore oriole took up residence in an elm
at the edge of her lawn. My friend and her husband
watched as the oriole and its mate began work on the
graceful hanging nest for which this bird is justly famous:
a soft purse woven of plant fibers, skillfully draped from
the twigs of the elm.

"Then we had an idea," she told me. "We placed the phonograph near the window so the oriole could hear. We put the record on and played his song."

The result was startling. When the recorded song burst out, the oriole stopped in his tracks. He looked around to right and left as if he were trying to figure where the call came from. "Then he flew off through the trees as fast as he could go," my friend said, "with his mate about a hundred feet behind. And we never saw him again."

My friend couldn't tell, of course, what the recorded oriole was "saying." Quite likely the message was, "This is my lawn." Amplified electronically, it must have staggered the poor bird in the elm tree.

That was in the middle of May. Now, as June arrives, there's a change in the songs of the birds. You can recognize the difference even if you can't tell a crow from a cardinal. This, the marked slackening of the torrent of sound from the trees and bushes, tells that the birds are preparing for summer.

It was long thought that a major function of bird song was to attract the attention of enemies searching for the female on the nest. Now it is realized that the male's flashy colors, as well, serve in this regard. Coupled with his bold antics, these colors distract predators from the difficult task of finding a quiet female, often dun-colored, hunching motionless on a dun-colored nest. So the decrease in song may have little relation to the safety of the bird or its mate.

More likely, the birds are singing less because the need for song has lessened. A male no longer needs to win a mate. Nor is his song required any further for another function it serves in many birds: to stimulate the flow of female hormones that, in turn, trigger the maturity and release of the eggs. Also, with his rivals established in territory of their own, he does not find his home boundaries in constant jeopardy. Since he thus sings less frequently, his neighbors are not prompted into song, either, and the whole countryside quiets down.

I once saw how this latent capacity to sing could burst forth again when needed. A friend and I were hiking on a dusty gravel road in early June. It was almost hot, by Vermont standards, and not a bird was singing in the late-morning sun. Suddenly, as we drew abreast of a thicket of birches and alders, the woods came alive with sound. A flood of flutelike notes poured out from perhaps a hundred feet away. It sounded as if half a dozen wood thrushes were singing at once.

Cautiously entering the thicket, we discovered that this was, indeed, what was happening—except that our half dozen thrushes were, in reality, only three. But they were engaged in such a spat, singing and fighting and chasing each other, that it sounded like twice that number. The result of the conflict was delightful to our ears, even though we realized the birds were not singing an avian trio, but three separate solos. Apparently they had met where the corners of three territories joined, precipitating a bitter—though melodious—flare-up of old rivalries.

Occasional outbursts such as that of the wood thrushes remind us that the birds are still around, although less vocal. Actually, their total numbers have lessened as well. A large portion of the flood of sound during the first three weeks of May is the contribution of the warblers. Sweeping from as far south as South America, they pass through our woods and fields by the thousands. They chatter and chirp and buzz and whistle and sing. Each of some two dozen species has its distinctive call—from the husky "bees-bees-bees" of the golden-winged warbler to the jubilant twittering of the Canada warbler that reminds me a bit of a canary. The hordes of these songsters are gone by Memorial Day, however—some to travel as far as the tree limit in northern Canada. With their disappearance, the woods seem even quieter by contrast.

There's still another reason for the lessening of song. Peg and I learned of this on watching a pair of bluebirds that nested in one of our bird houses. We timed the visits of the bluebirds to their family of four flourishing young ones. Every two and a half minutes, on the average, one parent or the other arrived at the nest box with a generous supply of insects. To hunt up all that food must leave little time for song.

Not only have bird songs diminished, but the relationship between species has altered, as well. This tells that more change is taking place. A familiar example of this transition can be spotted almost anywhere in America: the abrupt turnabout in the attitude of the birds toward that feathered rascal, the crow.

Earlier in the spring the crow was simply an oversized bird, sharing the woods and fields and pastures with its neighbors. Appearing in our front yard some late February morning from its sheltered winter haunts in the valleys, the crow perches in one of our big maples. Sometimes it drops down to the feeder for a bit of suet or a table scrap. The smaller birds make way and allow it to have the pick of the food, but that's about all the notice they give it.

In March and April, crows wander over the awakening fields with the redwings and starlings and grackles in noisy, amicable assembly, gleaning what food they can find. Mourning doves, horned larks, sparrows, and finches may join the throng, appearing scarcely aware of the presence of their large neighbor.

Now things are different. Spring is coming to a close.

That sugar maple tree in which the crow perched so in-nocently may hold something more than leaves and limbs and trunk. Couched in a fork is the mud-plastered nest of a pair of robins. The nest represents a whole series of events: a long migration, spirited fights for territory, the wooing of a mate, and the sheltering of three or four eggs against enemies and weather. To have those blue eggs catch the sharp eye of a crow is to invite certain disaster. Hungry crows make short work of the eggs and young of other birds.

The robins rise to meet the crow. By their shrieks and cries they proclaim the passage of the seasons: the honey-moon of spring is over, as it were, and there's a summer family to be raised.

Launching out, the robins drive the crow away before it has a chance to alight in the tree. They chase it and dive at it, scolding and hurling dire threats. As they reach the edge of their territory, the cry is taken up by the next robins, who give a similar reception. And thus the fugi-tive crow is passed from one set of irate birds to another. Redwings and kingbirds may even alight on its back and spur the clumsy flier to greater efforts with a few vindic-tive pecks.

Like as not these are the same birds that deferred to the crow on the spring feeding grounds. But now right-eous indignation is on their side. And so the crow flees in haste, leaving behind a trail of smaller birds drifting vic-toriously back to earth.

Not always does the battle go to the just. A crow may accidentally alight on the ground, perilously close to a bobolink's saucerlike nest, or the domed-over cradle of a meadowlark in the grass. Immediately the crow is set upon by a pair of protective parents. Instead of hastening to escape, however, the intruder merely flies a short distance, apparently to test the reaction of the birds. If they slacken their efforts, he turns toward the original spot. Then, walking instead of flying so his smaller adversaries cannot take advantage of their nimbleness in the air, the crow continues exploring and "sounding out" the distracted parents. It is almost some kind of grim avian version of the game of button-button, where the searcher's adversaries tell him he's getting warmer or cooler. But this "game" is played with the lives of baby birds instead of an inanimate button.

I watched such a performance in a distant meadow through my binoculars. It took a crow less than five minutes to zero in on the nest of a red-wing blackbird in a clump of grass. There, ignoring the attacks of the blackbirds, he reduced their home to a shambles. When I arrived on the scene ten minutes later, I found that the nest had contained only eggs, however, so most likely the blackbirds would build again.

Sometimes the crow itself becomes the defender, when protecting its own young. While hawks and owls are never lightly dismissed by crows, their presence in winter and early spring is grudgingly tolerated. In June, however, the crow sets up an outlandish squalling the minute a hawk appears on the scene. The commotion summons other crows in the vicinity. Soon the hawk is the center of a diving, caterwauling rabble. Long before it can get close enough to damage a nest, the hunter is met and turned away. Between those wide-ranging red-tailed hawks over Mt. Abraham and several isolated groups of crows, there is a feud that may break out at any time all summer.

With such raucous, sharp-eyed relatives protecting them, fledgling crows probably have little to fear. But the parents take no chances. Fortified by the protective urge that increases enormously in birds when there are mouths to feed, the crows challenge almost any large bird. They will even tackle the single real menace fierce enough to swoop down on that nest of twigs in a tall evergreen—the great horned owl.

Horned owls have been known to carry off skunks and domestic cats. They have even snatched hats off the heads of astonished hikers. But when an owl is confronted by a delegation of crows, out to protect their nests, it flees to the deepest woods.

Thus the birds announce the coming of summer. Not with spring songs, nor with courtship displays, nor battles with others of their kind. Summer is the darting of a needle-beaked hummingbird toward that freebooting nest robber, the blue jay. It is a sparrow's whirlwind pursuit of a female cowbird who may have been trying to leave her egg in the sparrow's nest. It is the screaming dive of the common tern right at my face as I pick my way through its rookery on an island in Lake Champlain. In short, it is the boldness—indeed, the desperation—of living creatures to protect their own, now that the promise of spring has become a reality.

When a bird was sitting on a clutch of eggs, she might desert the nest rather than face a determined enemy. Most birds can lay more eggs as needed. Now that the eggs have hatched, the stakes are higher. The female has far more attachment to living young than to inert eggs, and she goes to great lengths to protect them. I recall a female black duck—normally one of the shyest of the whole tribe of ducks and geese—suddenly bursting forth from the grasses near my canoe on a Massachusetts marsh. Crying piteously, she flopped in the water as if in her death throes.

Her act was so convincing that I was tempted to follow her. But I checked the impulse and looked around. I discovered that I had accidentally trapped her between two steep-sided points of land, and my canoe formed an effective barrier to her escape. And soon my gaze made out the reason for her behavior: several black-and-yellow ducklings floating like fluffy corks beneath the overhanging grasses, looking at me with bright little eyes.

Backing the canoe away, I opened the gate, as it were. But the black duck would have none of a headlong escape. Her struggles brought her almost within reach of my paddle. I allowed myself to be taken in by her antics, and she lured me out into the main stream of the marsh. The farther we got from those ducklings, the more rapidly she went through the water. Soon I was paddling at a good speed to keep up with her. Finally, when I was at a safe distance, the mysterious affliction suddenly left her. She sprang effortlessly into the air and vanished over the trees.

The broken-wing, wounded-bird act is familiar to nearly everyone who has spent time in the outdoors. Fewer people have had the chance to witness a similar performance in the mammal kingdom. Sometimes it involves a tremendous amount of courage on the part of the actor. I recall one day when we were getting our little summer cabin ready for my cousin and her family. As the children and I were sweeping and cleaning, Peg called us to the bureau where she was working.

Huddled in a nest of old rags and paper were five young white-footed mice. This gentle species seldom bites even when full-grown, so I reached down and picked the entire nest out of the drawer. Then I carefully cradled one of the squeaking young in my hand.

While we were inspecting its large tissue-thin ears and great dark eyes, Peg suddenly nudged my arm. Wordlessly she pointed to something on the floor. It was the female whitefoot, come to claim her brood. Sitting up on her haunches, tiny pinkish-white paws clasped like hands, she was the picture of motherhood emboldened in asking for her own.

I lowered the youngster to the waiting mouse. Without hesitation she took it in her mouth and scampered away. A moment later she was back again—and again and again —until she had claimed all five of the mouselings. Thus this tiny creature, who ordinarily would have fled at the first sound of our footsteps, was attesting to the surge of summer through all two ounces of her.

I know of a red fox who, with equal disregard for the risks involved, stood barking at a traveler on a country road. She held her ground while her pups made their escape over a stone wall. Her act was so fascinating, however, that the pups turned and watched, once they had gained the safety of the wall. There they stood, with five pairs of ears pricked forward—as much absorbed in the vixen's performance as was the hiker who told me the story. Finally, in what must have amounted to a wave of frustration, the vixen leaped the stones herself, reprimanded the pups with a good cuffing, and sent the whole tribe packing through the bushes.

With growing babies to protect, a cottontail rabbit will actually rush from her hidden nest to attack a wandering house cat. Our dog, Rebel, was chased through the woods by a female whitetail deer—Rebel frolicking around and around in great high spirits, while the doe snorted in her efforts to strike him with one of those lethal hoofs.

If the month had been May, the doe would have fled, probably before Rebel was aware of her presence. Her fawn, lying alone and perfectly still, would have been safe because of its spotted camouflage and almost total lack of odor. Now, in June, however, the awkward youngster could probably no longer "hide" in plain sight on the forest floor, so its mother rushed to protect it.

The common bats tell that summer is just around the corner, too. Earlier, when these flying mammals first ventured out on the balmy evenings of April and May, their flight was buoyant and effortless. Now their airy, dodging strokes are a bit more labored. The female bat carries her young around as she flies, and the added weight of even the single youngster borne by our common little brown bat can be a handicap in the search for food.

Luckily for the hard-working female bat, her insect food is more plentiful now. Many insects complete an entire cycle from egg to adult in a few weeks. Where there was one moth or gnat or beetle in April, there may be dozens of the same species in June. They are exact duplicates of the adults that preceeded them, and they seem bent on populating the world with more dozens of their young. Indeed, without the bats and the birds and similar fortunate circumstances (or unfortunate, from the insect point of view), the entomologist's prediction might come true: a single pair of houseflies and their progeny could cover every continent on earth to a depth of forty-seven feet in a year.

There's a new source of insect life now. This is the host of species that are true creatures of the summer. They are just beginning to appear. Your window screen on these warm evenings is bombarded by a bungling, shiny-brown beetle about the size of a grape. If the beetle gets into the room it sets out on a collision course with the nearest electric light. After a jarring crash, there is silence. Then the rustling of scratchy claws tells you it's climbing up for another wild flight around the room. The "June bug" has arrived.

Focus a magnifying glass on the June bug. Train your

lens on the shining body and the antennae with their terminal segments shaped like an opened hand of cards. You may see something vaguely familiar, if you recall your ancient history or literature. The clumsy insect under your lens is a true scarab, distant cousin of the armored beetle revered by the Egyptians and immortalized in Poe's story "The Gold Bug."

The June bug is also called "May beetle," since it's common to both months. Buzzing through the darkness of the next few weeks, it seeks out a mate. A few days later the female lays several hundred eggs. Back into the darkness of the soil go the tiny grubs, to spend a year in the world underground. When the season comes full circle again, there lies a new June bug on its back on your living room floor. As it waves its feet in the air it carries the message that summer has come.

Then there are those soft-bodied beetles known as fireflies. About the middle of June you see the first twinkles as the males take wing. They are searching for the females which, in some species, are flightless and known as glowworms. These, in turn, will produce glowworm larvae. By the Fourth of July the air of the meadows will be glittering with silent fireworks equal, in their way, to the noisy display of rockets and flares overhead.

Much about the lives of fireflies remains a mystery, even though people have been curious about them for centuries. Many fireflies glow independently of others about them, but a few flash in unison. How the signal is passed from one end of a field to the other is not known. If it were a simple case of one flash triggering a response from its neighbor, a progressive wave of light would be expected as successive insects take a brief moment to react. There is no visible time lag, however, even in a large meadow. This has led some scientists to speculate that the eyesight of fireflies is far more sensitive than previously thought: a momentary glow by any individual may be perceived by hundreds of others at the same time, triggering a mass reaction all through the air of that summer night.

The way in which the glow is produced is also a question. Although it is known that it involves a chemical, luciferin, which is combined with oxygen to produce the familiar light, scientists have been unable to duplicate the process in the laboratory. Giving out almost all its energy in the form of "cold light," luciferin is far more efficient than our incandescent bulbs, which squander energy as heat. Even fluorescent tubes hum and become warm and struggle along at a fraction of the efficiency of the familiar, unknown glow on the after-section of a firefly.

Apparently the light of fireflies serves to bring the sexes together. Here, too, there are some questions. How do males and females recognize each other in the brief instant of a flash in the dark? How can a male of one species be sure he is approaching a female of the same kind? And, in species with wingless females, how does the male distinguish his flightless mate from an equally-flightless larva?

Positive recognition is important. Although they seem gentle and harmless, fireflies and glowworms are carnivorous. They may attack a potential victim in an instant. A case of mistaken identity could well be the last error one of these insects would ever make.

There are only half a dozen species of fireflies likely to be found in a given area. They could scarcely be called abundant, as insects go; few people have ever seen one of these creatures close at hand. Yet each little meteor, shooting through the darkness, is an event in itself. By its uniqueness it serves to emphasize the unseen hosts, the multitudes, the veritable ocean of a quarter-million insect species in America. This ocean is forever building up and lapping at the bulwarks of the natural world each summer.

Occasionally your most casual glance will pick out a ripple or two in this flood of insect life. Touch the curled leaf that sheltered a few dozen aphids earlier in the spring. An apparently new insect jars loose and flies off through the air. It is the winged form of those same flightless aphids of a month ago. Now, with every speck of leaf surface occupied by the sucking insects and with the twig faltering in its ability to supply food for them all, the situation is desperate—for both twig and aphids. Something, obviously, has to happen.

Here is where those airborne aphids play their vital role. Hatched, apparently, in response to the plight of the entire colony, the winged insects depart for some distant leaf. Often they carry the fortunes of their species with them. Their earthbound sisters, tight-packed and unable to move, will soon face starvation on that overcrowded twig.

Alighting on an uncluttered leaf a few inches—or half a mile—away, the gauzy-winged pioneers begin a new colony. And some unfortunate plant, scot-free until now, provides the larder to be riddled by the pointed beaks of a few hundred more plant lice, wingless and pear-shaped once more.

Looking a bit like aphids with their piercing beaks, but only remotely related to them, juvenile water striders also give witness to the advent of summer. You may look straight at them without even realizing they are there. Hatching out by the score, the gnat-sized striders gather together and form living rafts on the water. Such a raft may appear to be merely a floating bit of gray chaff the size of a platter. But let a mosquito fall into the water and the raft breaks up into hundreds of bold little pirates. The striders' sharp beaks make quick work of the mosquito— or even a large moth—when its struggles have ceased.

Like many other aquatic insects, water striders can take to the air and escape from a pond or stream as it dries. Among the vertebrates, the eel and the catfish choose a different route, slithering from one pond to another over damp grass on a rainy night. Thus the appearance of any of these creatures, seemingly out of its element, may be a sign that summer has arrived at a nearby waterhole. By forcing a general exodus the weather creates a stream, not of water but of creatures searching for water.

Even the tadpoles, hatched from the eggs of those frogs you heard earlier, have a built-in escape mechanism. All through April and May they have developed, scouring the algae from submerged objects around them and darting to the bottom whenever a shadow appeared over their pool.

In early June a menace may approach that is greater than dwindling food or threatening shadow. Perhaps the sun has been unduly hot this particular year and the pool has shrunk alarmingly. Now it is drying up.

Within ten days, say, the last of the water will be gone. This means the fishlike tadpoles have only that much time to turn into land-dwelling frogs. Their flapping tails and soft bodies will be helpless on land. Somehow they have to compress a month or six weeks of adolescence into a quarter of that time.

And this is just what they do. The dwindling area of the puddle and the increasing frequency with which neighbor bumps against neighbor gives warning of impending doom. The faltering food supply makes haste imperative and the higher temperature of the shallower water makes it possible: the tadpoles begin to exchange yesterday's tails for tomorrow's legs.

Hour by hour the tissue of the finny rudder of each tadpole is resorbed into the bloodstream. Thus the tadpole has extra material available within itself even if food disappears entirely. The tail substances are redeposited now as little buds—to become bones and sinews and toes, first of the hind legs and then of the front. The little pucker mouth widens. The tadpole begins to porpoise up to the surface every few minutes for a gulp of air. The eyes grow and bulge into the periscopes that will serve their owner so well. In a few days the rounded contours of the tadpole (literally, "tail-head") have given way to the head and shoulders and trunk of a frog.

And quite a frog it is. Still bearing the stub of its life-saving tail, it hops away from the remains of its pea-soup aquarium. It scrambles out of sight into the grass—an independent mite that sometimes is scarcely bigger than a fly. It made its deadline with hardly a moment to spare. Behind it, on the drying mud, are scores of little gray spots—the carcasses of other unfortunate tadpoles whose only mistake was to hatch a day too late.

Some scholars think the invasion of frogs in Biblical Egypt may have been a host of ex-tadpoles dispossessed by a severe drought. To give such an explanation, of course, takes nothing from the importance of that event. Anyone who has seen the myriad young toads and frogs that leave the water normally each summer cannot fail to be impressed. Give them an outsized plague of flies to feed on, and you might have the makings of a twentieth-century invasion.

In ponds with enough water to withstand the approaching dryness, there's more of a changing of the guard than an exodus. The little spring peeper quits the water in late May or June, abdicating in favor of his equally vociferous cousin, the green frog. This dour musician will continue his banjolike clunking until well into July, while the peeper will have disappeared except for an occasional reminiscent chirp from the forest. There, clinging to leaves and twigs with adhesive discs on his toes, and with his tan body marked with a brown X as perfect camouflage against the bark, the peeper fits his scientific name exactly: *Hyla crucifer,* "The wood spirit who bears a cross."

The trees themselves are adjusting to the shifting season. Scientists tell us that modern man seldom lifts his eyes more than fifteen degrees from the horizon. Thus he rarely notes what goes on above his head. Our forbears of a generation or two ago lived much closer to nature and were more aware of the changes in the forests of early summer. In fact, my grandfather used to gauge the time to plant his entire crop of corn by the size of the hickory buds.

Corn, it seems, can be ruined by the slightest frost. Nevertheless, gardeners try to plant their corn as soon as possible in hopes of an early crop. And here is where the hickory trees come in. Their large buds develop slowly, no matter how enticing the weather. So the overenthusiastic farmers of my grandfather's day would be sobered by the hickories. "Plant your corn," they'd say, "When the hickory buds are as big as a crow's beak."

This sounds like double-talk until you recall that the crow's beak was all too familiar to those farmers. Most farmers would shoot a crow or two if they could. Then they would hang the carcasses up in the cornfield as a warning to the others. It didn't work too well, but it gave a certain sense of satisfaction. The pointed buds of the hickory would be the size of the pointed beak of the crow—or the length of the last two joints of your little finger if you didn't have a crow handy—about the middle of May. The hickory leaves themselves would be fully expanded in early June.

The discarded scales from the buds of those late-wakening hickories filter down through the branches to the forest floor. There they may come to rest on the blackened leaves of hellebore, jack-in-the-pulpit, dogtooth violet, spring beauty, and scores of other short-lived plants. These residents of the forest understory have to be short-lived, many of them, as the leafy canopy will soon throw the ground into dense shade. The smaller plants steal their moment in the sun while they can. Then they disappear, except for their vital berries and bulbs and seed pods, just before the foliage above closes off the sunlight.

Summer, of course, brings scorching temperatures. A tree or shrub anchored in one place can scarcely flee from the blistering heat as an animal can. So it crams most of its development into a few short weeks after the earth is warm. Then let the soil bake as it will—the tree has achieved its major growth.

It is this hurry-up-and-slow-down cycle that leads to the familiar growth rings in trees. Foresters refer to the light, softer areas of each ring as "spring" wood. The rest of the ring—darker, denser, often narrower—is sometimes called "summer" and sometimes "winter" wood. It was laid down when the tree was at the slow point in its annual career, which may encompass nearly eleven months of the year. The wider band of spring wood may have been formed in three or four weeks. Cut on an angle, these contrasting zones lead to the grain in wood and show graphically that, even while rejoicing in spring, as it were, the tree is laying a foundation for the trials of the summer ahead.

Herbaceous plants, springing up anew from the soil each year, get a somewhat later start than their wood-bearing relatives, but even here there is a struggle for that vital foothold. Although any summer day bears witness to its quota of plants just springing into bloom, most of these have been rooted and growing for weeks, even months. The August goldenrods that turn our north meadow to sunshine got their start back in June. We can identify aster and gentians, too, by their leaves months before the first blooms appear.

It is thus with the majority of other herbaceous plants, as well: the leaves and stems, at least, struggle into being as fast as possible in spring. By gaining a foothold while the growing is good, they can hang on during the dusty heat later, when growing conditions are poor.

Plants that have already blossomed before these late June days are growing fruit and seeds. But even their early maturity takes the summer into account. Few new seeds, indeed, will sprout if planted now. They need summer's dryness to enable them to ripen and mellow. Only after long months of aging can they be germinated. Thus the seed-bearing parachutes that blow from a dandelion head or the brown nuggets that scatter from a withered buttercup are only beginning their careers. Far from being termination, summer is another step in their growth—and a vital one.

Long-lived plants that must stand in the snow from one year to the next have to look forward beyond the summer at hand. There is another winter ahead. Preparations for this faroff season have been made, too—almost as soon as growth began in the spring.

And such preparations may save the day, especially in our New England with its unpredictable weather. Often in May—sometimes as late as June—a great breath of chilly evening air may descend from the lands to the north, bringing a killer frost.

With the earth not yet warmed up to serve as a giant heating pad, the plants are at the mercy of the cold. Crystals form on their leaves and sparkle under the stars, for a late frost almost always occurs on a clear night. There are no sheltering clouds of an overcast sky to prevent the day's heat from escaping. Crisp and erect, the plants are stealthily ravished by the cold.

The next morning the sun quickly melts the frost. But the damage has been done. Microscopic needles of ice have formed in the tissues by the billions, puncturing the membranes of the delicate new cells. By midmorning the green of yesterday's leaves is replaced by darkening browns and blacks of frost-blighted foliage. That afternoon the landscape looks as if swept by a forest fire.

Yet the trees and the shrubs and the sprouting plants are equal to the occasion. At the base of each leaf, and down below the soil on each tender plant, is a tiny bud. Under ordinary circumstances these little growing points would mature slowly through the summer, to form the winter buds of the following autumn when the leaves had fallen. Now, however, they are called into action. They've experienced an abbreviated "winter" of a few hours. Faithful to their built-in destiny, they swell and grow, just as they would a year later.

Within a week or ten days the shocked brown of the countryside is replaced by hopeful green. New ferns unroll their fiddlehead croziers up through the shrunken wisps of last week's fronds. Axillary buds burst into greenery from the bases of the blighted leaves. The warm sea-

son was forestalled a few days, that's all. Now it is back
again. The average date of that last devastating frost in
our little mountain town is the second of June.

At least the threat of frost is past, even here in northern
New England. Latent buds have sprung into use as
needed, and tender tissues have toughened for the hot
weeks ahead. "Broken" wings and legs have been
dragged all over the countryside by birds and animals in
protection of their young. In many cases the offspring
themselves have been introduced to this new season—a
lively procession of skunks, for instance, that paraded
through our garage one evening, or a family of ring-tailed
raccoons that romped through our new flower bed like a
troupe of clowns.

Even though our calendar says it's only the middle of
June, a world of plants and animals has turned its back
on spring. In their lives it is already summer.

To prove it ourselves, we have only to glance to the
east, to the air high over Mt. Abraham. There is our red-
tailed hawk, her golden eyes piercing the forest below as
she seeks food for her own two downy young—our wheeling summer sentinel in the sky.

4

"Me, Too!"

THERE is something that appeals to me about plants and animals that take half the season to get going. I warm to them on several counts.

First, they interest me just because they are late. Tardiness is so human a trait. I feel a kinship, somehow, with the tree that develops foliage along with its neighbors but doesn't get around to the Big Day of blossoming until July. The bird that keeps putting off nesting reminds me of a bachelor friend who bewails his singleness—but hasn't taken the obvious cure even though he's now in his forties. And the toad that waits for just the right summer night to lay its eggs brings up a picture of the timid driver at a stop sign while traffic rushes heedlessly by.

Secondly, these late-season laggards have an excuse for being the way they are. There's a reason behind the poke-along schedule of each seeming dawdler. And to find that reason is, almost always, to discover an interesting story.

Then, too, a number of the living things around me are just now getting to flower or build nests or have young, as the case may be, because of another circumstance familiar to humans—they have had to stand in line. In a few cases this is literally true: a creature must wait on the scene until things fall in place.

If you have been fortunate enough to discover the nest of a ruby-throated hummingbird you have witnessed the end result of such a wait. This tiny bird, scarcely as big as your thumb, often uses the fuzz of the cinnamon fern for nesting material. Thus, to find enough of this preferred substance, it must bide its time until the ferns have developed. Flying into a clump of fern, the hummingbird seizes a mouthful of fluff. Then it takes the fluff to a horizontal limb where its mate is waiting. Together they shape the wispy material to the body of the sitting bird.

When enough fern material has been gathered, the hummingbird speeds away for an even filmier substance —the web of a spider. Finding the proper cobweb, the bird uses its unique ability to fly backward as well as forward, darting in and out as it appropriates the silk of the unfortunate arachnid.

After several spiders have been dispossessed, the hummingbird has fashioned a nest lined with flannel and covered with silk, as it were. Now the bird adds the finishing touch: flecks of gray-green lichen. The completed product looks like a bulging tree knot the size of a Ping-Pong ball, camouflaged with lichen and sheltering two white eggs no larger than peas.

Another bird that seems to take forever to nest is one of the most spirited creatures to liven the country scene: the American goldfinch or wild canary. The goldfinch spends the spring and early summer flitting about the fields like a butterfly, apparently without care for tomorrow. Months ago the males swapped their olive-gray winter coats for sunny yellow breeding plumage with black wings, tail, and forehead. Then, while most of their feathered neighbors applied themselves to raising a crop of young, the goldfinches played among the spring and summer flowers. As they sprang upward in their airy, bouncing fashion, they looked like a handful of dandelion blossoms that had suddenly taken flight.

At last, with the thistles and other flowers going to seed, the goldfinch gets around to building its nest. Now it becomes clear why the bird has been holding back. This cheerful mite fashions a nest as much of sunshine and summer air as the bird itself. One of its favorite nesting materials is thistledown—until now a scarce commodity indeed. It also uses delicate plant fibers now available such as are found on maturing seed pods. It weaves these, together with the tenderest grasses, into a soft cup in a bush or the outer twigs of a tree.

A change then comes over the goldfinch. The female becomes furtive and shy. She steals to the nest daily, laying an egg each time until five or six are produced. Then, covering their blue-whiteness with the sombre yellow-green of her own body, she settles down for nearly two weeks of waiting.

The male assumes a new role. Now he has a duty to perform. Like most finches, the goldfinch is a seed eater, and he fills his innards with the seeds of ripening weeds. Flying by a devious route to his hidden mate, he regurgitates a cropful of seeds into her waiting beak. Quietly he makes his exit, then flies to the top of a nearby tree and serenades the world with a liquid, gurgling babble. The melody of the goldfinch is one of the few bird songs you will hear in August.

When the young hatch, their food demands keep both

adults busy. They, too, are fed on seeds, moistened and softened in their parents' crops. It has been estimated that a burgeoning goldfinch family may consume ten thousand weed seeds daily for two weeks. Such a steady stream of food necessitates a bountiful supply. The goldfinch had to postpone nesting until July or even August, when all those seeds were ready.

The cedar waxwing is another late nesting species. This is a neat brown bird with black chin and forehead, plus a perky crest that rises and falls according to its mood. The waxwing gets its name from the odd tips of its secondary wing feathers, as if each had been dipped in red wax. It is known as the cedar bird or cherry bird because of its fondness for cedar berries and wild cherries.

Like the goldfinch, the waxwing feeds its young by regurgitation. Berries and small fruit are in best supply during July and August, and the parents bring a throatful of pulp, seeds, and an insect or two to the nest every few minutes.

The capacity of those clamoring youngsters is astonishing. In fact, on one occasion, it was alarming. We had trained our telescope through an upstairs window on the nest of a pair of these birds in the bushes below. We watched in approval as one parent brought enough blueberries in a single trip to feed three of the five young waxwings. Soon it was back with another load. Four minutes later the process was repeated—three generous helpings while we watched.

This, we told each other, must have amounted to at least a handful of blueberries in seven minutes. Then the thought hit us both at the same time: where were they getting all those blueberries?

We have a dozen cultivated blueberry bushes that ripen their fruit from mid-August to September. Early in

August we cover them with cloth netting as protection against the birds. Obviously there was a hole in the netting somewhere. There were no wild blueberries close enough to furnish such a ready supply.

Entering the enclosure, we began to look for a break in the netting. Yes, there was the break. And there was the culprit—all five of him. Two robins, a catbird, a purple finch, and a brown thrasher. But no waxwings, at least for the moment.

We chased all those freeloaders out through the door of the enclosure and fixed the hole. Then the birds were forced to subsist on such prosaic foods as chokecherries, wild raspberries, and luckless insects. Peg and I kept a closer eye on our crop, picked it as fast as it ripened, and boiled up a batch of blueberry jam almost in self-defense.

In this latter part of summer, not only the business of feeding but that of homemaking may have its special problems. There always seem to be a few optimistic birds —or maybe they are down on their luck, and have lost one nest after another—that try once more for a crop of offspring. But the impulse to raise a family is likely to get supplanted by the migratory urge at this late date. When this happens we get a call to babysit some foundling whose parents have deserted him.

We have thus hand-raised a purple grackle, two red-winged blackbirds, a song sparrow and—I must confess—a couple of starlings. They come to us, all voice and mouth and appetite, as late as the first week of September.

These P. S. Babies, as Peg calls them, seem to be more common among birds than among other creatures. Doubtless this is because birds may stay with the same mate for the entire season if the first nest is not successful. Reptiles, amphibians, fish, spiders, and insects may make a brief alliance, and that is that. Among the mammals, despite their watchful care of the young, a lost litter may not be replaced for an entire year.

This is the usual scheme of things. Sometimes, however, even the orderly schedule of the mammals becomes confused. Last Labor Day weekend a lady from New Hampshire called to tell about a baby raccoon whose eyes were just open. I judged he was about four months behind time. Another caller from a school in Connecticut wondered what to do about two abandoned baby gray squirrels "who can't even climb out of my sister's doll carriage, Mr. Rood."

I turned the lad and his late litter of squirrels over to a high school biology teacher who, I hoped, would be suitably grateful—and who would encourage an early release for the squirrels as soon as they were ready. Squirrels make engaging subjects for study, although they are too lively to be confined. Besides, wild animals should not be kept captive. When released, they cannot take care of themselves.

Like many other rodents, squirrels may produce more than one litter a year. Hence, some segment of a parade of juvenile mice, squirrels, muskrats, and flying squirrels is apt to trickle across the bridge to our house all the way into October. They are transported here by the contrite owners of overzealous cats and dogs or by some youngster who had plinked a female "varmint" with his air rifle just in fun—and had watched the unhappy creature die in earnest. Others of Peg's "P. S. Babies" among the mammals have included young hares and rabbits, three frightened opossums delivered to me on Long Island after I'd given a talk, and an occasional hungry baby shrew.

I've never been able to save the shrews, which are

sometimes captured as they follow the mother, single file, nose-to-tail, on her endless search for insects. Shrews burn up their food so fast that they are starving by the time we receive them. We've had better luck with most of the other mammals. These late-edition waifs show as much zest for life as their older brothers and sisters, even though they will have to grow up fast in order to be ready for winter. Fortunately there are briar patches, brush piles, and tired old farm buildings around our place, so each autumn's foundlings can wander off at their own good speed to spots of their own choosing. Over two decades Peg and I have thus aided in the fortunes of more than a hundred birds and animals.

Those three opossums, by the way, stayed on Long Island. As the species seldom gets into northern Vermont, we gave them to a local zoo rather than haul them off to an uncertain fate.

While many animals are tapering off their reproductive season there is one group that is just getting under way. This is the order of mammals known as the Chiroptera— literally, "Hand-winged"—the bats. No sooner has the female unburdened herself of her current progeny and begun to fly freely once more than she starts in on next year's offspring. The red bat mates as early as August; the other bats a few weeks later. Occasionally you may see a pair of courting bats performing dizzy aerobatics in the evening sky, or even coupling in a sort of airborne lockstep as they join in mid-air.

Time between mating and birth in bats may be eight months or even more, but this is a misleading figure. The sperm is received by the female and kept in a small receptacle in her body through the winter months. Only after sperm and egg unite—sometime in late winter—does development of the young begin. So, I suppose one could say that the bat, instead of being half a year late in mating, is really a half a year early.

The female bat bears from one to four youngsters, depending on the species. When ready to give birth in May, she hangs from a tree in such a way that the babies are delivered into the membrane that stretches from her tail to both hind legs. There she holds the young until all are safely born, like a housewife carrying objects in her cupped apron.

There's another of my wild neighbors that finds late summer a good time to start a new generation. It's an astonishing creature that hops about on two hind legs like a kangaroo. Covering eight to ten feet in a bound when really pushed, it yet has a body length of only four inches. This animated pogo stick is known as the jumping mouse.

Actually, there's a six-inch tail as well. The tail serves like the feathers of an arrow, guiding the creature in its leaps. The jumping mouse can even twist its tail and swerve in mid-air—an impressive sight, to say the least. To come across one of these creatures in woods or meadow is to swear your eyes are playing tricks on you. The mouse is like some kind of a frog in fur, rapidly leaving your alien presence in astounding hops.

Many mice mate at will from spring to late autumn, but the jumping mouse—especially the woodland species —seems to have two breeding periods. One is in the spring and the other is in the latter part of summer. Thus it's a perfect example of Peg's P.S. Babies. Three or four youngsters are born about a month after mating.

Although I've seen a number of the adults, I have stumbled across just one jumping mouse nest in my lifetime. And I'll not soon forget it. I almost stepped on the nest, a grassy affair at the base of a little bush. A mother and several halfgrown mouselings bounced away in different directions. It was as if the lid had flown off a pot of giant, brown popcorn.

Jumping mice are the most accomplished leapers among mammals. If we could jump as far for our size, a six-foot man could cover two-thirds of a football field in a single bound. Or, comparing weight for weight, he could jump more than three miles.

These mice are opportunists when it comes to food, as are many of their rodent relatives. They are not above taking a spider or caterpillar along with their fruit and seeds. And the choice of such living food varies from day to day.

Some kinds of crab spiders, for instance, are just now beginning to appear. The crab spider makes its home in a flower—oftentimes the flower of one certain species. Gaily-colored like the petals, it lurks with open arms until a bee or other insect comes too close. A snap of those arms, a quick stab with numbing fangs—and the victim ceases to struggle.

Crab spiders come in many colors: yellow ones, white ones, even zebra-striped ones. Some have warts and bristles that camouflage their shape. Their outline may resemble that of a flower part—an anther, perhaps, or a pistil. One spider that frequents our raspberry blossoms looks disarmingly like nothing more dangerous than a bird dropping.

A spider in fancy colors would be an easy target for enemies before there were flowers against which it could become invisible. The spider, however, is equal to the occasion. Its outer skin, or cuticle, is transparent. Through this transparent layer can be seen the color of the intestinal canal with the food it contains. Thus the spider, after having fed on a green or brown insect, becomes green or brownish itself, protected by the color of the latest victim showing from within its body.

As the season advances, small pigment cells beneath the transparent cuticle grow to maturity. They screen out the colors of the spider's internal organs while imparting the camouflage it will wear as it lurks among the flowers.

Some crab spiders merely postpone hatching from the winter egg until blossom time is at hand. Then, when the goldenrod or butter-and-eggs or hawkweed comes into bloom, the juvenile crab spider obligingly climbs right into the middle of it.

Many are the insects and spiders and other creatures that must wait their turn. Very seldom is anyone stung by wasps or hornets before July, for instance. Only the queen wasp lives through the winter, and it takes weeks for her to establish a new family in the spring. Even then, a small colony of wasps is much less apt to sting an intruder than is a large colony. Apparently there is boldness in numbers—a trait possessed by humans, too. Hence, the peppery insects are more even-tempered in July than in August, say, when the population of their paper city has been bolstered by several hundred of their younger sisters.

One wasp, far smaller than our hornets and yellow jackets, actually stands in line. It is a tiny creature, scarcely larger than the period at the end of this sentence. This wasp, *Pteromalus*, spends its juvenile life within the pupa of the cabbage butterfly. Gardeners view the butterfly with alarm, as its green caterpillars consume their broccoli and cabbage and brussels sprouts.

The tiny wasp flies from plant to plant, following the scent of one cabbage worm after another. It investigates each and eventually finds what it is seeking: a caterpillar about to form its chrysalis. Then the wasp takes up its position a few inches from its intended victim and settles down to wait. It may wait hours, even days. Eventually the unsuspecting caterpillar ceases to eat, huddles in a favorable spot, and prepares to shrug itself out of its larval skin.

When the chrysalis has forced its way out of the caterpillar coat, the little wasp moves forward. An egg in just the right chink of that rapidly-hardening armor—and a new generation of wasps is on the way. Thus this parasitic insect, a link in one certain chain of living things, is able to assert itself only after the previous links have been forged. And since the wasp's role in the drama has consumed much valuable time, each egg splits into a score or more of equal parts. From each of these parts a new wasp will grow.

Almost any creature occurs at a certain place and time because it fits there better than at any other. Seldom is this more wonderfully portrayed than in the annual return of one of America's most famous insects—the orange and black butterfly called the monarch. The caterpillar of this handsome species lives on milkweed. Hence its other name, by which it is known to farmers and school children the country over: milkweed butterfly.

The monarch is a migratory species. It spends the winter in southern climates, sometimes as far south as Florida and the Gulf Coast. Millions of monarchs overwinter in the town of Pacific Grove, California. Their clustered thousands have resulted in butterfly festivals, special protective city ordinances, and the establishment of a Butterfly Park where they can rest undisturbed from their long flight south.

When winter is past, the monarch takes to the air once more. Pushing north with the strengthening sun, it may travel dozens or hundreds of miles—depending, partly, on how much energy it has left. Descending to the tender new shoots of milkweed, it leaves an egg here and there on its return journey. And at some point, especially for the monarchs with the farthest to travel, those sturdy wings finally beat their last.

But the northward journey is not over. The migration merely pauses. The eggs hatch into caterpillars that feed almost constantly on the milkweed leaves. They nourish their green-and-black banded bodies for a week or more until they are full grown. Ten more days in the pupal stage, and a replica of that original butterfly reappears in a score of places—its wings now fresh and untried.

Now the migration is resumed. Perhaps the final destination of that particular family requires another pause while more bodies, exhausted, drop to the ground and more larvae grow to maturity. Such, indeed, may be the case with the monarchs that finally arrive here in Vermont. They—or, rather their forbears—may have left their winter quarters in the deep south before spring had officially arrived on the calendar. And now, on these July and August days, the long journey comes to its end.

These latest butterflies mate and produce eggs like the monarchs before them, but a new guiding force enters the lives of their young. Up until the official start of summer, varying around June 21, the days had been lengthening. Then came the summer solstice—literally, "sun standing still." The solstice marks the other extreme of our planet's orbit around the sun—directly opposite the winter solstice around December 21, when the amount of daylight is at its least. When the last generation of monarchs gets its wings in September, the daylight is waning steadily. Now the migratory urge is reversed. The newly emerged butterflies turn their backs on the fields toward which their parents struggled so recently, and follow the sun south for the winter, as it were.

Day length plays a part in the fortunes of the plants, as well. It might seem that these long hours of sunlight would bring any plant into flower, but such is not the case. Try to get a July blossom on a chrysanthemum, for instance, or a dahlia or cultivated aster or salvia. You'll have little if any luck. These are all "short day" species, requiring ten or more hours of darkness. They produce fine foliage but no flowers until the daylight lessens. On the other hand, your lettuce and spinach "bolt" into bloom almost while you look at them. They are "long day" plants, and their blossoms thrive on the early dawn and long hours of daylight—as do corn, clover, gladiolas, and delphiniums. Less fussy species may bloom almost anytime: tomatoes and carnations and those dandelions in your lawn.

It's the unexpected that makes the seasons so interesting, just as opposites lend variety and spice to our own lives. On a particular late-summer day the green of your lawn or meadow sports a little white sphere that grows within a week from the size of a lemon to that of a basketball. Cutting through its leathery skin, you find the pallid globe to be soft and mealy-moist within. You are in the presence of one of the fastest-growing fungi on our continent—the giant puffball.

The real growth, however, has been taking place in the soil from which the puffball sprang. Spreading down and outward for many yards in all directions in the earth is a network of fine mycelial threads. They probe like microscopic fingers, growing, expanding, consuming the nourishment in decaying organic debris in the soil. All spring and summer they have been exploring from one food particle to the next, actually binding soil granules together by their network. Thus the puffball grows in a fashion similar to that of its small cousins, the mushrooms.

Now, at long last, the fruit of all that labor shows itself. The arrival of a puffball signals a feast for insects, mice, squirrels—and people. Edible and delicious, a chunk from a ten-or-twelve-pounder is a meal in itself. As each one comes along, Peg and I slice and fry a few slabs of it in butter. But for best results we try to use only the newly-developed puffballs. Soon that white interior turns yellow and, eventually, brown with billions of spores. When fully mature the spores fly away on the breeze if the tissues are squeezed—hence the name puffball.

The puffballs, along with the rest of the plants in the meadows and forests nearby, are performing on cue. The tulip tree in my parents' yard in Plymouth, Connecticut may bloom as late as July. So does the only wild Vermont specimen I know of that almost forgotten forest giant, the American chestnut. This lone tree is probably still healthy because it is so far from possible infection by others of its kind.

Following instructions sent down through a million generations, in spite of the blight that killed its ancestors, this single chestnut tree goes through its annual rites. On or about my birthday—July 7—it faithfully raises long, creamy-yellow catkins to the sun, even though there is not a single living tree of its species within miles to share its triumph. Fortunately it is self-fertile, so each year it produces a half-bushel of nuts—half the size and far sweeter than the imported chestnuts sold in stores.

With a little woodland sleuthing you may discover a chestnut or two of your own at this time anywhere east of the Mississippi. Although the old trees have largely vanished, the stumps continually send up sprouts from the roots. Every now and again a sprout withstands the blight long enough to produce blossoms. You'll recognize it in an instant from those long, slender strings of flowers. Its leaves are distinctive, too—up to ten inches long, strap-shaped and with saw-toothed edges.

Besides, this remnant of the once-mighty forest giant will probably be the only tree in bloom in July. In more ways than one, the American chestnut is at the end of the line.

Now that the chestnut is in bloom, the spring parade is largely finished. Most of the mating and flowering and birthing has taken place. But not all of it, by any means. Even first cousins vary widely in their response to the call of the seasons. The shrub known as Bridal Wreath (*Spiraea prunifolia*) lavishes the perfume of its flower-laden branches on the June air. Its close relative, the tough little hardhack or steeplebush (*Spiraea tomentosa*) chooses the other end of summer.

The hardhack's woolly leaves may spread themselves for weeks in the hot sun before the tiny pinkish flowers appear. These flowers are arranged in the erect spire that gives the plant its pious-sounding name. And steeplebush may blossom right up until frost.

There are late bloomers in the aquatic world, too. The waters of the New Haven River in front of our house run cool—or cold—all year long. In spring the river rocks are green with winter algae. They are still green now, but summer mosses have taken the place of the algae.

The water has receded, too. Whole new populations of snails, insects, flatworms, and roundworms live in the dampness on the emergent rocks. Their self-contained little world is frequently inundated as a playful wave of the river sloshes up on the moss and lies half in the sun, half in the water. There these denizens, just now appearing as if out of nowhere, feed for a few weeks on the moss and bacteria and each other. Then they are gone for another year.

This stream is also the home of the little fish known as the black-nosed dace. The dace have been schooling together all spring and early summer in mixed company, apparently unaware of the presence of the opposite sex. Now, however, they seem to discover *la difference*. The belly fins of the males turn blood red, and the fish become quite adventuresome. When the heat of the sun drives us into the refreshing waters of the river—and those refreshing waters drive us shivering back out into the heat of the sun—the dace nip at our bare feet as we stand on the gravelly bottom.

Black-nosed dace spawn in July and August in these mountain streams. More southern varieties of the species gain a month or two in the warmer weather. But their earlier spawning does not guarantee better survival, for the eggs of dace are eagerly sought by predators—even by other dace. Luckily those strands of moss and the rough nature of the rocky bottom guarantee that some of the eggs will be hidden. Then in a few weeks we see what my sister and I used to call "pinfish." These are young dace, swimming in schools of several dozen individuals, whose numbers assure that a few of them will survive to nibble on somebody's toes next year.

Another fish that spawns in July and August in our clear streams is the freshwater sculpin, or miller's thumb. It is a grotesque little scamp that seems all head and fins and no body. The miller's thumb is a fearless creature. During the breeding season it is downright pugnacious. I have been attacked by these three-inch warriors and have had them follow me right up to shore. One even came halfway out onto the wet sand in his efforts to vanquish the finger that I waggled at him.

Even with such fearsome tactics on the part of the

male miller's thumb, the eggs may not last long enough to hatch. Glued to underwater stones by the female, they are guarded by her mate with such vigor that he may chase an enemy clear into the next pool. While he's gone, other predators have a field day.

The river has other denizens that seem late but are really right on time. We find the cast skins of stoneflies on the sun-baked rocks in midstream. These insects are cousins of those early spring stoneflies that wander over the snow, but this species emerges in August. Even later relatives may come out clear into October. Mayflies, too, despite the common name that refers to their occurrence in spring, have species that do not emerge until the time of frost. As Ann Haven Morgan wrote in her *Field Book of Ponds and Streams,* one may expect mayflies at almost any time and aquatic situation "except foul water." This was back in 1930, when the word "pollution" was virtually unknown.

These mayflies-in-August are typical, in a way, of all the thousands of Johnny-come-latelys that impart their own special stamp to the latter half of summer. They fit a precise niche that opens up in time and space. In many cases the "why" or "how" of this niche escapes our feeble observations. Until you get to know these plants and animals they may seem tardy—or at least choosy—with their late flowering and nesting and their maverick ways of life. The few we have looked at, perhaps, have an excuse for seeming to dawdle: opportunities must open before they can proceed with their particular way of life. Or, to put it another way, those lives may have become fitted to opportunities that opened again and again, over eons of time.

But what of the other late comers? Are they tuned to the sound of a different drummer in their own lives?

Quite likely, if they have survived all this time. It was

long a mystery, for instance, what governed the egg-laying period of a certain Spadefoot toad of our Great Plains. One year it might lay its eggs with the other amphibians in June. The next year it would stubbornly refuse to visit the pools with the rest of its goggle-eyed relatives, but might wait almost until August.

Then, finally, the "drummer" was found—one that made perfect sense in the watery world of the tadpole. The Plains spadefoot postponed egg-laying until 3½ inches of rain had fallen after the average temperature had risen to 52°. Though it had no thermometers or rain gauges to help it along, the spadefoot somehow sensed the time when there would be sufficient water in the temporary pools for its quick-growing young to survive.

All of which, I suppose, suggests that terms such as "early" and "late" are strictly human concepts. Or, as the naturalist Henry Hill Collins, Jr. suggested in contemplating the spadefoot's low-geared breeding season, some creatures have to be smart enough to go out *into* the rain.

5

Fall Crescendo

Sometime in July I hear it. It is a thin, wiry buzz, so frail that it seems more imagined than real. Often it first comes to me when I'm driving along with the car windows open—a hint of sound from the weeds along the highway, lost in the simmering heat at sixty miles an hour. If I'm walking along a country road or out in the meadow, I may try to zero in on the whisper as it rises and falls. Advancing cautiously while the sound floats on the air, standing still when it stops, I may be lucky enough to discover its origin: the first grasshopper of autumn.

Until this time the grasshoppers have been silent. Most 'hoppers begin their generations anew each year. Hatching from tiny sausage-shaped eggs in the soil, the nymphs look like caricatures of grasshoppers: almost all head, ridiculous little bodies, and wings that are merely flattened buds along their backs. Wings are the special property of adults, and among this most tuneful of insect families nearly all the music is produced with their aid.

The new-hatched nymphs are ravenous. Scarcely larger than a grain of sand at first, they concentrate on leaves and blades of grass as new and tender as themselves. Stuffing themselves by the hour, they are soon too large for their skins. Splitting the confining jacket, each 'hopper quickly swells to a new size and goes back to its eat-hop-eat routine. Its body is more streamlined and those wing pads slightly longer with every moult.

After half a dozen such leaps into life the grasshopper reaches the last moult. Shedding its skin for the final time, it climbs on a blade of grass. Its wings, now fully formed, soon dry to parchment in the summer sun. Then, if it's a male, it rubs its scratchy thighs against those sandpapery wings and buzzes its exalted status on the summer breeze.

Soon its solo becomes a duet as another male reaches maturity. They are joined by more of their species—and by their cousins, the crickets and katydids. Gradually the meadows and roadsides take on a new dimension of sound. Although your calendar may declare it's still July or early August, the performers are getting ready for the great symphony of September.

At this time the music of the grasshopper family will serve merely as a backdrop against which other early autumn actors go through their paces. Later it will become the main event. Sweep an insect net through the grass now and you'll get twenty nymphs for each adult; do the same thing next month and the proportion is reversed.

Why do the insects sing? If you have walked through an overgrown meadow in late summer you know how the grass is alive with leaping crickets and grasshoppers that fountain up with every step you take. It seems impossible that such a jumble of insects could be organized into singing territories, like those of the birds. Yet, among some of the songsters at least, this is actually the case.

Stridently affirming its presence in a series of rapid twitters that sound like a runaway sewing machine, a male coneheaded grasshopper lays claim to a swaying stalk of goldenrod. Aphids and flies and beetles travel there unmolested, but other male coneheaded grasshoppers are sent scurrying. Thus each male establishes his own little sphere, within which will come the whirlwind of courtship and mating and egg laying in the weeks ahead.

A cricket guards his territory—the few square inches immediately adjacent to his special clump of grass—by scraping one raised wing against the other and creaking defiance to interlopers. Indeed, so scrappy are crickets that the sport of cricket fighting has been practiced in the Orient for centuries. One hand-raised insect is pitted against another, with the wagers flying as fast as the leaps of the miniature gladiators.

The song attracts the female even as it warns other males to go find their own grass blades. And in the song of the snowy tree cricket—that monotonous high-pitched trilling call you hear in so many summer-night scenes in movies—there is more involved than simply music. Beneath those raised wings of the male are two glands that secrete a substance whose smell and taste are relished by the female. Thus when the snowy tree cricket sounds his call he is also wafting his perfume on the early autumn air. If he's successful, he'll keep other males at bay until some unattached female takes the bait, as it were. Often he goes right on singing even while she tastes the insect aphrodisiac. Sometimes he may win a second female, as well.

The tree cricket is marvelously adapted to its surroundings. Alert to every suspicious move, the little white insect has been able to make a living for itself in the improbable world of gray tree bark and green shrubbery. It is exquisitely tuned to the temperature of the day as well. Like other insects it moves faster when it's warm than when it's cool. The monotonous *trr! trr! trr!* of the male speeds up on a warm night in direct proportion to the temperature. Count the number of trills in a fifteen-second period. Add forty, and the sum will be within a degree or two of the thermometer reading.

Nor is this all. Even as the male offers his inducements to the female, the snowy tree cricket is keenly aware of the other males around him. He sings in perfect rhythm with his rivals. Now and again he drops out of the chorus, but when he rejoins it he picks up the "beat" of all the others. Thus a brushland or hedgerow may throb with what seems to be the call of a single giant tree cricket. Even if you get in your car and speed past such a field, the insects are in such perfect timing that you apparently hear just one musical note over and over as you whiz along.

Crickets and grasshoppers and katydids welcome the coming autumn with song. This is to be their season, just as spring was the time of the frogs and summer the time of the birds. And if you turn your back on the fields and steal into the woods on these August days you will hear other sounds that mark the approach of fall.

Even though the leaves have not yet turned color, a few have curled and dropped to the ground. There's a whispering among them as the earthworms maneuver the leaves into their hidden burrows, stem first. The ever-active chipmunks are more audible now, too, as they scurry through those fallen leaves for the half-bushel of nuts and seeds they are storing against their fitful winter sleep.

If luck is really on your side, you may hear a racket

that stops you in your tracks. It's a percussion sound: a crashing, splintering noise as if someone were beating the life out of a small bush.

And that is just what is happening. If you're in deer territory, the noise is that of a buck rubbing the velvet off his new antlers, thrashing them repeatedly against an unfortunate sapling.

In other surroundings the noise could be a bull moose or elk, preparing his adornments for the fights and struggles of the mating season. Right now the antlers are ragged with old velvet, but the male will soon rub them to a high polish. The shrubs and bushes that bear the brunt of his attack will present a sorry sight for years to come. There's a sugar maple tree in the woods behind our house that grows from a single trunk like a candelabra—the result, no doubt, of the concentrated attention of a white-tailed buck with itchy antlers half a century ago. The trunk, crushed to the ground, has sprouted along its entire length.

Game poachers, looking for venison out of season, sometimes call deer within gunshot by rattling a stick in the bushes. A buck hearing the noise may trot to the scene, spoiling for a fight.

A change comes over the doe as well. Still accompanied by last May's fawn, she now lets it be known that the youngster can no longer look to her for milk. Instead, he has to learn to browse on twigs and other greenery of the forst, or feed with her among the clover and alfalfa of a meadow.

Once I saw a fully-antlered buck chasing a doe along a woodland trail while her twin fawns followed uncertainly a few hundred feet to the rear. When she circled around in such a way that she drew near them, they joyously galloped up to meet her, but she struck at the nearest with her front hoof. Finally the whole procession disappeared over the ridge: doe, buck, and fawns—the latter at a greater distance and more hesitant than ever. They had grown up the minute their prospective stepfather entered the scene, whether they wanted to or not.

The deer's lumbering woodland neighbor, the black bear, performs his own rites of autumn. Several times Peg and I have come across a stump or old log in the woods, torn asunder and strewn over an area big enough to park a car in. This is the work of the bear, expending effort seemingly out of proportion to the food value of the grubs or ants he seeks in the rotting wood. In his determination to add to that "saddle"—the reserve layer of fat along his back—he gobbles up all manner of edibles and not-so-edibles: roots, berries, mushrooms, insects, old bones, and even an occasional stick or pebble that catches his fancy.

If he discovers a hive of bees, the bear will spend an entire day clawing his way to the honey, despite the assaults of the hive's outraged residents. Nor do the hot-tempered inhabitants of a hornet nest deter him from ripping the paper palace apart to get at the succulent larvae within. The bear's heavy coat protects him against the hornets, even though he leaves the area in a fine state for the next passerby.

Bear families do not separate in fall, as do those of many mammals. The female gives birth every other year, so the cubs traveling with her may be a year and a half old and nearly full-grown in size. Coming across the tunnel of a mouse or chipmunk, such a platoon will tear up an area half the size of a tennis court, if necessary, to get to the rodent's nest.

The bear's small cousins, the raccoons, have less permanent family ties. The adolescents now part company with their mother. They, too, store up plenty of fat. Free-wheeling along like Halloween merrymakers, the young raccoons investigate every source of potential food, sometimes with devastating results. They can reduce a corn-field to a shambles in one night's work.

If a raccoon comes to a stream and feels about beneath the bank, it may discover a crayfish. Snatching its prize and placing it on land, the raccoon rolls the crustacean around like a wad of dough. It may reduce the crayfish to something resembling a ball of shredded coconut, so as to avoid being nipped by those pinchers.

Raccoons are the very soul of cleverness. They leave no stone—or tin can—unturned in their effort to lay in a good store of fat. A friend of mine recalled four raccoons that visited her uncle in the Adirondacks. "They kept raiding the back porch garbage can," she told me, "and they tipped it over every time. Finally we anchored the can to a wooden post. Now that it couldn't be tipped, they had to climb down into it. The three biggest got inside, but when little Number Four tried to crawl in he was knocked off the edge. Finally he climbed the post and backed successfully into that can full of animated fur."

Along with the raccoons in the universal urge of youth to explore, half-grown rabbits and weasels and wood-chucks roam the countryside, seeking possible living space. We've even had young chipmunks snooping into our kitchen in August when the screen door didn't close.

The trees overhead—especially the old, hollow ones—become the new homes of young flying squirrels. They venture out on their own after a summer spent gliding through the woods with their soft-furred mother. Once they've established themselves in an old woodpecker hole, their curiosity may get the best of them if you scratch on the bark. Few sights are more appealing than that of an inquisitive flying squirrel peering down at you with its large, expressive night-vision eyes, in response to your "knock" at the base of the tree.

Able to eat almost any plant or animal food it can find, the young flying squirrel will spend the winter in its new-found territory. Gray squirrels, for their part, are busy harvesting the first nuts and acorns as they fall. Sometimes, with what seems almost human impatience, they'll snip nuts and seeds, still unripe, from the limb. Then, scooping them up, they haul them off to storage. These fresh-cut treasures, lying on the ground where they have dropped, are a sign that autumn is almost here.

The "wings" of sugar maple and ash and box elder seeds flutter down on your lawn chair. They tell of a busy squirrel, hidden in the branches above, who is trimming his food before he stores it.

Mushrooms begin to appear in unusual places. Nipped from the ground and carried aloft by squirrels, they are hung in the crotches of twigs to parch in the sun. When dry, they can be stored for months without spoiling. Evenly the deadly *Amanita* may be harvested and cured, its wispy remains apparently no longer harmful to the durable rodents.

Those same trees that furnish the bounty for the squirrels may hold out a semaphore that signals the passing of summer: a leaf or branch colored with the hues of autumn. It stands out conspicuously, a red or yellow flag against the green of the rest of the tree. Scientists still are not sure as to what triggers this early change, but it's a hint of the season to come.

If you look further, you'll find another sign of the times. Even the greenest of leaves is scarred and gouged. After the first of August it's hard to discover a leaf that hasn't fallen victim to a pest or blight or some other woe. The only perfect leaves, almost, are those that have just emerged—some late-sprouting plant, or the new green of the farmer's clover, ready to be cut for the third time. Most of the rest of the foliage has done its job. Now it serves as a playground for the latest generations of grubs and caterpillars and beetles.

These pests are having their day. The birds no longer scour the trees and bushes so diligently; they have no clamoring mouths to feed. Besides, many birds are in the midst of their post-nuptial moult, swapping those bright summer hues for the more somber ones of winter. The moult apparently is something of a trial, even if it takes place a few feathers at a time. The bird is wary, subdued, seldom venturing out into the open.

A number of birds have already gone south. The red-start, that active warbler whose orange and black makes it look like a half-sized oriole, is no longer present to scrutinize the twigs and foliage. By mid-August it has left for its winter home in South America. The red-eyed vireo, ceaseless summer soloist who sometimes sings with its mouth full of caterpillars, has likewise departed. Oven-birds, wood thrushes, bobolinks—some of the most vocal of our summer visitors—have disappeared. Although we welcomed them eagerly when they arrived, we scarcely note their passing.

Each bird follows its own pattern. "Our" barn swallows are also "their" barn swallows—"they" being the residents of Brazil and tropical America. Scores of these blue-coated birds with the forked tails hold their conventions on the power lines along our little country road in late August. Then, after a week or two of apparently endless indecision, with false starts and constant bickering, the big day arrives.

They drop from the power line for the last time. At ten o'clock on September 7, say, you can count a hundred barn swallows. And at 10:05 there's not one to be seen. Though the actual date may vary, it's Capistrano in reverse.

Southward the swallows go, through the insect-laden air. Scooping their flying prey on the wing, they can make good a part of their route as they eat. Finally, weeks after they depart the sunny fields and yards of almost every section of North America, the swallows arrive at their destination. Swiftly driving on pointed wings, they swoop down to gladden the heart of some child as far south as Buenos Aires.

"Look!" he cries, as the orange breast of a graceful bird catches the sunlight, "*Las golandrinas!* Our swallows are back!"

So it goes, over and over. My mother and father in Connecticut begin to get the little slate-gray juncos at their bird feeder in October. These may be the same birds that left their Green Mountain home here in Lincoln in August. In mid-September the Canada Geese begin to fly their squadrons across our sky, leaving both Vermont and Connecticut behind as they head for the Virginia marshland.

Sometimes, when we go beachcombing along our Atlantic Coast, Peg and I see the bird with the greatest wanderlust of all—the Arctic tern. Its whole life consists of getting the jump on the seasons. Breeding above the Arctic Circle in May and June, it scarcely has time to teach its young to fly before the whole family turns south. By the time we spot it on an August visit to Cape Cod it has already traveled a thousand miles.

This black-capped fisherman with the immaculate white breast and tail will continue south, plunging into the water after its food all the way to the southernmost continent of our globe. There, as Peg says, you could just as well call it the Antarctic tern.

A few weeks in the Antarctic are all it can spare. Soon it's on the way north again. Since it spends both ends of its journey near the poles at the time when the sun hardly sets, it probably sees more daylight than any other living creature. And in the process it makes a round trip of twenty-two thousand miles—to say nothing of the miles it flies in its daily coursing over the water for unwary fish.

I remember once when my son, Roger, bemoaned the departure of a family of Baltimore orioles. We'd been watching them in their woven hammock swaying at the end of a maple branch over a river. "Why do they have to go south anyway?" he asked. "Why don't they stay here all winter so we can feed them, like the chickadees?"

In the minds of many scientists who have studied migration, the answer may lie in a sort of geological memory. The ancestors of the migratory birds were forced south by periodic ice sheets which invaded the northern hemisphere. When the ice retreated, they came north again. Now, some ten thousand years after the last glacier, they may still be following the old, old pathway. So perhaps the Arctic terns and the house wrens and the whooping cranes and the hummingbirds are going back to the good old days without knowing it.

I used to wonder why we didn't see more birds as they headed for the southland. There are at least two reasons: many migrate at night so they can rest and feed during the day, and many fly so high we couldn't see them anyway.

Radar screens have picked out large flocks at more than ten thousand feet over Illinois. Here in Vermont we often hear ghostly chirpings as the birds call to each other in the dark far above our heads. Sometimes our binoculars pick them out as their legions appear briefly against the face of the moon.

The migration of the hawks has a pattern of its own. Powerful though they are, they are also heavy-bodied and depend on favorable air currents for their journey. Circling in a thermal, or current of air rising from the heated land, the hawk allows itself to be carried aloft. I have watched hawks ascend, scarcely flapping a wing, from treetop level to where they were but specks in the sky. When the thermal finally cools and tops off, losing its lift, the hawk sets its course southward in a long glide. Then, finding another thermal, it repeats the process. It may travel half a hundred miles in a day with scarcely any effort.

Those invisible thermals, so important to the hawks, often rise so high that their moisture condenses. Then each thermal is evident by the cap it wears: a fleecy white cumulus cloud, sitting on top of this rising column of air.

The fluffy, almost complacent appearance of the cloud belies the turbulence within. A cumulus cloud contains a jostling, whirling miniature cyclone. Indeed, if the currents are strong enough, the innocent-looking cloud becomes a dark thunderhead. Within this thunderhead may be crystals of ice that rise in the updrafts and fall back again, only to repeat the process. As they travel up and down, they attract moisture in concentric layers like an onion, eventually becoming hailstones. The rushing of the winds, shattering water droplets in the cloud, and the energy involved in hailstone formation in the chilly air create a great charge of static electricity. Lightning plays through the clouds. The thunder roars, and a good storm is in the making.

Finally the air can no longer support the hailstones. They fall toward the earth. Usually they melt before they strike, but sometimes they rattle down in a fusillade that shreds the leaves of trees, shatters windows, and even kills animals. Hailstones as large as baseballs attest to the terrific power of the winds that held them aloft—perhaps as much as two hundred miles per hour.

Pelting the earth, the first raindrops make little craters in the dust. If the rain falls too fast, the dust particles fly around and seal up the pores in the soil. The raindrops roll around in this dust without wetting it, like little puddles of quicksilver. Then the deluge flows rapidly over the parched earth, scarcely soaking in at all but forming rivulets that turn into temporary streams. These tumble headlong into the regular streams and rivers, and the main content of the thunderstorm—sometimes two or three inches of needed rainfall—may flow uselessly out to sea.

Such cloudbursts may provide much of the rainfall in the arid west, screened from the moist Pacific breeze by the coastal mountains. But not always are the results of cooling so violent. Here along the Atlantic seaboard the more gently rolling land serves as a ramp to raise passing breezes until they, too, lose their moisture.

In summer our own Mount Abraham sports a topping of cloud about one day in six. This becomes one day in four as the upper air cools in early September. There are many days when the wispy cap is indistinguishable from the general cloud cover, and some days when the four-thousand-foot peak disappears completely. Rain from such overcasts is gentle, penetrating, soaked up, and held by the grateful plants and soil. The porous land, shot through with the tunnels of fifty thousand earthworms per acre plus the cavities left by root decay, is like a giant sponge. It holds water so well that rain may fall all night with scarcely a rise in our streams.

The moisture in the soil builds up as a water table beneath the surface. Finally the water table rises to the level of little valleys and depressions. Last spring's pools and the intermittent "Sometime Streams," as one of my friends calls them, come back to life. Our small pasture brook, dry since late June, returns to its flowing, bubbling self in September. And with the general rise in water level, aquatic life quickens as it, too, prepares for autumn.

Predatory water insects take to the air again. They scatter themselves over these new pools in search of the reawakened life that has remained dormant through the hot months. Water snails creep away from the dry weeds where they have cemented themselves, dissolving the glassy protective film from the mouths of their shells. Tiny crustaceans burst from their summer eggs or make their way out of watery prisons in the mud. Aquatic earthworms untangle from the living ball where they had woven themselves together to conserve moisture. Within hours of its rebirth, each pool again swarms with life.

In the deeper ponds and lakes a different sign marks the coming of autumn. This is the seasonal overturn of the water. Water, like most substances, contracts when it cools, becoming denser. With the slight chill of the nights and the retreat of the sun a bit more toward the south each day, the surface layer of water cools and becomes heavier.

Sinking, the chilled water displaces the lower layers of warmer water, which rise to the top. They, in turn, become cooled. The process continues until the whole pond is thoroughly stirred, top to bottom. You can see the result of the overturn as the water becomes murky and muddy from the movement of this giant mixing bowl.

Now comes an interesting question. If colder water becomes heavier, why doesn't the coldest water go down to the bottom and remain there—eventually becoming ice far below the surface? And how can the entire pool warm up in spring if warmer water floats on top of cooler water?

The answer lies in an amazing property of this unusual liquid. As water is cooled, it becomes denser, true—but only until it reaches 39° F. Then, if it's cooled further, it begins to lose density again. Thus when the temperature of the water is just above freezing, it is lighter in weight than it was at thirty-nine degrees. Hence it rises to the top once more—there to freeze into ice. And in the spring, as it warms toward the magic thirty-nine degrees, it sinks again.

Scientists feel that most life on earth owes its existence to this unique behavior of water. Other liquids are densest when they are coldest, but ice will float no matter how cold it is. Hence it is there at the surface in the spring, ready to melt back into water again. If it sank it would lie forever as a great inert mass in our lakes and ponds. The only available water would be the thin layer that formed on top of this ice for a few weeks each summer.

And so we gaze at the murk of the late-summer overturn, complaining that it spoils the visibility of fishing and that it makes swimming like taking a bath in cold dishwater. Scarcely do we consider that this overturn is nature's way of preparing the ponds for winter—and that, without it, there'd be no fish to catch and no fisherman to catch them. No dishwater either, for that matter.

Early autumn is the time the young beavers in our woodland pond strike out on their own. About the size of a squat-legged cat, each half-grown kit follows the watercourse to a new location. There, alone or with the help of another, it builds a dam of mud and sticks and stones to form a storage pond for its winter food supply.

Beavers of all ages lay up food by jamming young hardwood saplings, butt first, into the mud of the pond. Poplar, or aspen as it is often called, is the favorite. As long as the sapling is fully submerged it will remain fresh and green for months. So now, with an entire winter ahead, the beaver sets about preparing for the cold weather to come.

In spite of popular opinion, America's largest rodent is hardly "busy as a beaver" until this autumn urge sets in. It spends much of the summer leisurely inspecting its dams, nibbling at pondside greenery, or just loafing. Only if a sudden flood bursts a dam or if its pond is drained by highway workers who see the rising water as a threat to their roadbed, does the beaver live up to its reputation. Then a determined family of these furbearing engineers can outstrip a man with a shovel—the man digging at the dam all day and the beavers repairing it all night.

At this time there is apt to be another sign of activity at the pond. In summer the beaver seldom leaves its watery abode. Now, with a store of groceries to gather and with youngsters wandering in search of new homes, beavers are apt to stray many yards from the water. And this is when Peg and I scrutinize the mud—not for beaver tracks, but for the pawprints of woodland opportunists who visit the ponds in hopes of a beaver dinner.

Foxes and bobcats make frequent rounds of the pools. Neither of these predators is a threat to a healthy adult beaver in its own element. But an exiled kit exploring a little stream or forlornly wandering about the edge of its former home—that's something else again. And so the travels of the fox and the bobcat may be rearranged at this time so as to take them across the dam each night. Then we can spot the doglike prints of the fox or the more rounded traces of the bobcat—the latter readily identified because no claw marks are showing. Like its domestic relative, the bobcat keeps its weapons sheathed until they are needed.

The beaver's small cousin, the muskrat, also foretells the season. It will be active all winter, finding roots of cattails and rushes in the mud. Now it gains new energy after the summer lull, repairing one home and building others. New hogans of mud and reeds blossom forth until the marsh looks like an aboriginal village in miniature. Some of these huts are the work of the latest crop of offspring, who, having left the parental nest, proceed to carve out their own living—literally—with those yellow buck teeth.

In its search for a new home a wandering muskrat sometimes strays as far as half a mile from the nearest water. Crossing a highway, it may become a roadside casualty, adding to the early-autumn toll of young opossums, skunks, mice, and other mammals—all out to seek their fortunes. Their pathetic little bodies—forty to the mile in the ditches and weeds along a stretch of New England road that we studied in a college wildlife class—give tragic evidence that fall is once again approaching.

Restless mammals on the move find their counterparts in the insect world. Not only are those crickets and grasshoppers becoming more vociferous every day, but changes take place in the numbers of the creatures that share the landscape with them. One of these changes may have a startling effect on humans as well. A certain active —and completely harmless—insect in its new-hatched zest for life has the capacity to throw normally rational human beings into a panic.

The creature with this faculty for causing a stir is a familiar late summer insect: the male *Polistes,* or common northern house wasp. His is the first male generation after a long summer of worker females in the paper nest. Hatched up there under the eaves, the thread-waisted male has the same fighter-plane outlines as his intended spouse. But he lacks one device that has made his mate famous: he has no stinger.

A stinger is really a modified portion of the egg-laying apparatus. Thus, of course, the male is out of the running. Nevertheless, he'll raise his wings threateningly if you come too close. He will even go through stinging motions if captured, but it is all a sham. In no way can he sting.

The next question then follows: how can you tell the harmless male from the not-so-harmless female? Simple— just look him in the eye.

The male northern house wasp—and sometimes there are hundreds of them in early autumn—has light-colored eyes and a yellow forehead. His legs and underside are yellow, too. His fearsome mate, on the other hand, is uniformly deep chocolate in color. She seldom comes in close contact with humans in a building. She has flown around man-made structures all summer and is wise to the ways of doors and windows.

The male, new-fledged and inexperienced, blunders through any opening and ends up buzzing against the glass. If that glass happens to be a schoolroom window, he may sail out across the student body at head-level if molested—sweeping a score of panicky children before him in the process.

On these late-summer days there are also male bees and hornets, but their paths seldom cross ours. Male aphids suddenly appear among those packed multitudes on the belabored twigs, too. Male cicadas make the treetops ring with their long, piercing buzz, lasting a full minute or more. Add these to the September symphony of the crickets and grasshoppers—plus the background activity of myriads of their distant cousins of all sorts—and this is, indeed, the time of the insects.

For many of these creatures this time of year is only the beginning. It is like the fever of activity around a launch pad before the rocket is fired. Those males in their millions are here for one main purpose: to be ready and waiting when the eggs of the females are ripe. Once those eggs are fertilized and placed away for safekeeping by the female, the activity of millions of insects will cease for another year. Then—except for the handful of species that overwinter in the ground and in the mud and under the bark of trees—all the fluttering and singing will be locked in those tiny, immobile jewels that are the eggs.

Sometimes the "launch" is actually just that. One September afternoon we were coming back from Rutland. As we drove into the yard, Peg suddenly called out, "Hold it! There's a fire in the garage!"

I jammed on the brakes. A thin column of smoke swirled upward from the concrete floor. It appeared as if an oily rag was smoldering. But the floor was clean—or at least, as clean as such a place can reasonably be.

We got out and took a closer look. Our garage floor suffers a common malady: subsurface moisture. With alternate freezing and thawing, cracks finally develop. It was out of one of these cracks that the smoke was emerging.

Now we could see what was happening. The "smoke" turned out to be the winged adults of the common little brown ant. They were pouring out onto the floor by the hundreds.

Many were fat-bodied, sleek, honey-colored and nearly

the size of a housefly. Their filmy wings reflected rainbow colors as they caught the sunlight streaming onto the garage floor. Climbing to the slightly-tilted edge of the concrete they took off without hesitation, circling out into the open air. These were the reproductive females.

The winged males were more numerous. Dark in color, a sixth the size of the females, they sprang into the air as well. The wingless workers, about as large as the males, scurried in apparently aimless haste. They reminded me of a little dog, circling with excitement, waiting for his master to get dressed for a walk.

As soon as they were airborne, a change came over those flying brown ants. We could see it happen before they'd left the garage. A moment before, both sexes had shown one purpose: to get into the air. Now they joined in a spirited game of tag. This was the annual mating flight.

Only one male would be successful for each female, although many tried. One after another a female would go glinting into the sun, surrounded by two or three satellites and trailed by several more. And even as she arose, other females could be seen drifting back to earth in the driveway and on the lawn.

We looked at a few of the returnees. Usually they consisted of a mated pair, with the male still attached. In many instances he clung to his enormous spouse like a circus rider on the side or back of a horse. In other cases, however, he bumped along unceremoniously in reverse as she hurried to find a spot to start a new family, apparently oblivious of her burden.

As we looked about, we made another discovery. A second "smoke" arose from the base of a gladiolus plant in the garden. A third was only four feet beyond that. Other wisps of ants streamed skyward on the hillside behind the house. There were several out in the south meadow and a large one at the corner of our old barn. This was a concerted effort, made by scores of nests—and millions of ants—at once.

The air was filled with winged forms. If a male lost track of his intended, he struck out on his own. Soon he'd run into the flurry of another swarm, where he might have better luck. And thus cross-fertilization could take place.

This was an insect bonanza for winged predators. Robins, cedar waxwings, song sparrows, and phoebes dipped into the swarms and took their fill. A catbird, grounded perhaps from overeating, hopped along the driveway and picked tidbits from the grass at its edge. Dragon flies shuttled back and forth, netting ants with the basket made by their six bristly legs.

What triggers such a performance? How do all those colonies get the message to send out their reproductive queens—and their temporary kings—on, say, Sunday afternoon? Why not Monday or Tuesday? There's an advantage to the species in crossbreeding: undesirable traits get watered down by the more common normal ones. But who gives the signal?

Apparently it's the weatherman. As the colonies approach maturity in late summer, their reproductives appear. These potential aeronauts have a vague impatience for the sunlight they have never seen. They buzz their wings down there in the dark. But they must wait for that certain day. Often it's a day after a shower, with the temperature and the barometer just right.

Then, and only then, does some unseen gate swing wide at the colony's exit. Free at last, the reproductives pour out in their millions. The exodus may take only an hour or two, but in that short time the colonies over dozens of square miles will have accomplished their mission.

This aerial journey of the ants is an event whose beginnings stretch far back into time. On one flight long ago, a number of flying reproductives circled above a mastodon, perhaps, or a sabre-tooth tiger. In the whirlwind of mating a few ants blundered into a bubble of clear resin oozing from some primeval evergreen tree. Their struggles entangled them until they sank beneath the surface of the syrupy liquid. This liquid hardened and aged until it turned into amber—a brownish, transparent substance not unlike the handle of a toothbrush. In hardening, the amber preserved its victims intact.

Today, some forty million years later, scientists marvel at the preciseness with which that little tragedy has been recorded: legs, wing veins, even bristles on the bodies of the prisoners, easily visible under a hand lens. There are other insects, too—flies, gnats, moths, beetles. Closer examination shows pollen grains, lichen fragments, mold spores, tufted seeds—the whole spectrum of airborne life on that balmy day so many eons ago. Each of these aviators, doubtless, was abroad on its own mission: to spread its kind as far as possible by means of the wide highway in the sky.

There were even aerial spiders. Impossible as it may sound, they were flying through that ancient atmosphere as well. Not that spiders had wings then, any more than they have them now, but they had long since developed a means of traveling in the sky. Indeed, "flying spiders" are thought to go back to the time of the early dinosaurs, more than two hundred million years ago. And their mode of travel was so successful that they still use it today. Known as "ballooning," it is often employed by newly-hatched spiders of certain species as a means of escaping their cannibalistic brothers and sisters or for finding new homes.

We saw this ancient process in action one day in early September. As Peg and I were standing on the bridge, a small spider sailed past, six feet in front of our noses. While we watched, it steadily gained altitude. As it passed over the river, the sunlight caught its "balloon"—a strand of silk that stretched six feet into the air.

A few moments before, the little spider had climbed to the tip of some convenient twig. Pointing that tiny abdomen skyward, it had allowed a rising current of air to draw silk upward from its spinnerets. When the pull of the silk was strong enough, the spider had released its hold and drifted away.

The glint of another silken strand caught our attention. It was higher in the air, perhaps twenty feet above our heads. Then we began to see other threads, glistening, near and far. And as our gaze followed beyond them we realized that the entire atmosphere shimmered with the presence of thousands of these airborne adventurers. The sky had a silver glow, as from thin, high haze. Mt. Abraham, softened in a silky sheen, seemed to be ten miles away instead of only four.

"Goose summer," this time of year is often called by country dwellers. The name may refer to the flocks of geese shortly to wend their way south, but it also may be related to the delicate silken network of gossamer that hangs in the sky.

Our continent has no monopoly on such a venerable occurrence. During a visit to Germany I discovered that the September of the silvery skies is known as *altweibersommer*—"the old wives summer," perhaps referring to the floss spun into cloth by elderly women. And a Danish friend reports that in his native land those days of early autumn were known as *Flyvende Sommer*, or "flying summer," when thousands of spiderlings, embracing dozens of species, took to the air.

Although the flight of the spiders is the most heralded journey of its kind, the silken lifeline is not theirs alone. A Labor Day tennis match in southern New England had to be postponed because thousands of caterpillars were lowering themselves on strands of silk from the leaves of nearby shade trees. When each strand was long enough or the breeze strong enough the silk broke, setting the caterpillar adrift—right across the tennis court.

These little balloonists may float only a few feet before coming to rest again. Or they may rise on a favorable gust to travel for miles. Caterpillars and spiders have been collected on the top of the lofty Himalayas, as well as on the ice around both poles. They were found in the company of a number of flying insects—all frozen stiff. Doubtless the entire company had been swept high into the air until the winds of the upper atmosphere caught and carried them—perhaps for months—before dropping them again.

Barring such adversity, however, the winds of fate are not that risky. The vastness of the air is an ideal arena for the spread of all who can use it. The September sun shines down on midges dancing ten feet above a decaying log in a mating dance that concludes with a few thousand eggs in the rotting wood below. Swallowtail butterflies circle to the treetops, then set their wings in a long glide that may take them half a mile. Plants join the pageant, as well: the tufted seeds of goatsbeard, fireweed, wild lettuce, hawkweed and hundreds more—picked up by a playful zephyr and borne off to seek new lives of their own.

These airborne explorers of autumn form a thin canopy over their terrestrial counterparts. There is the gentle spotted salamander, for instance, who chooses this season to forsake its shelter beneath a mossy rock and take up residence in the damp cellar of some startled householder. Then I hear from the householder, who pleads with me to save him from "this ferocious-looking lizard, who must be poisonous." There is also the gray squirrel who sometimes travels miles in search of a new and better hollow tree—new and better for *him*, at least, although to us it seems like the one he just left.

Autumn is declared more emphatically each day by all those buzzing, flying, migrating, food-storing, seed-releasing plants and animals. Each moment hums with activity. On your lawn the excitement may be marked by redoubled efforts on the part of the chipmunk, who gathers every morsel at top speed, as if tomorrow promised a foot of snow. He pilfers sunflower seeds from your rejuvenated bird feeder at the rate of two quarts a day, if you supply the seeds fast enough. And it's with pangs of remorse that you scoop up his treasure when you find it under an old lumber pile during your autumn chores.

But you needn't worry about robbing the chipmunk. His industry is typical of the exuberance of most of life on these early-autumn days. He probably has two or three other caches somewhere else. Besides, he's a compulsive hoarder. In a few weeks he'll bed down on a favored mat of seeds and turn his back on the rest of his collection.

Then, like so many of these autumn revelers, he'll sleep through much of the winter, anyway.

6

Autumn Echo

WHEN Dave and Alison brought their new son for a late-September visit, we assumed that little Joshua would have a quiet weekend in the country. After all, auto travel along our road is so scattered that each passing automobile is an event. Even on a fall-foliage weekend like this one, more than a car a minute was practically a traffic jam. So our daughter and her family should get a good night's sleep. Other than these fleeting transients, our nearest neighbor was a quarter-mile away.

Our nearest *human* neighbor, that is. We hadn't reckoned on the wild creatures that share our hundred acres. And it was one of these that put an end to Josh's slumbers. Early Saturday morning a bird with a fine sense of rhythm announced to all within earshot that time was awasting. Although he had clung to summer until now, he was yielding to autumn at last. But he wasn't giving up without a fight. And the noise of the struggle as autumn entered his life woke us all at dawn.

One minute there was only the murmur of the river in front of the house and the sound of the countryside slowly awakening. The next minute a jackhammer let loose outside.

I sat bolt upright. "Good heavens! What's that?"

"I don't know," said Peg, "but *where* is it?"

The noise stopped, then started again. Now that we were awake, we both knew what it was—and where, too.

Our room is on the south side of the house. The noise was coming from the north side. Or, more correctly, from the barn roof on the north side, forty feet from Dave and Alison's window.

We crossed the hall to my study. The strengthening dawn showed us the culprit: a black and white bird with red cap and throat and pale yellow sides. Slightly smaller than a robin, it clung to the side of the barn. The bird was a yellow-bellied sapsucker—one of the noisiest creatures in the woods.

Taking aim at a great, loose piece of corrugated roofing, the sapsucker hammered a third time. The whole tin roof shivered to its blows. The clatter must have been audible at that neighbor's house a quarter-mile away.

Now it was Joshua's turn. He joined the sapsucker in a high wail, with all stops out. And so, at about 6:15 on what was supposed to be a sleepy Saturday morning, we were officially up for the day.

If this had been April, we could have expected such a performance. Lacking any "song" other than a squawk that sounds like an ailing cat, the sapsucker declares his intentions by whacking away on a good resonant object. In our woods this could be a metal bucket hung from a sugar maple in spring. Or it might be a resounding hollow stub. Several rapid knocks followed by three or four slow ones are equivalent, apparently, to a wolf whistle. They say "I'm here, and I'm available."

But this was October. The same sun that had called forth the mating urge in spring as the days lengthened was supposed to have subdued it in fall with the decrease in daylight. Nevertheless, birds are individualists and our blatant woodpecker had been slow to heed the signals. Hence the dawn tattoo: an avian farewell to summer.

That sapsucker's reveille was one declaration that autumn still had a ways to go. And you can find plenty of others, right up until everything freezes tight. Even with winter close upon them, there are scores of plants and animals reluctant to part with the good days of summer. They remind me of children who want to stay up and watch the late show on television. In fact, these laggards are themselves the late show.

Long after their conformist neighbors have played their parts and left the stage, the procrastinators are still taking curtain calls. Condensed into a few weeks of autumn, you can see a replay of summer. It's a wan, ghostly summer for the most part, but occasionally there's a performance that will startle you. Joshua's feathered alarm clock was such a one: the tin roof was probably the greatest kettle-drum the sapsucker had ever found.

The sapsucker's parting volley is echoed in the tuneful farewells of other birds. As I type these words on the day before Halloween, a song sparrow is singing a threadbare little refrain out in the blueberry patch. It's substantially the same tune he sang so lustily all summer from the cherry tree, but now it's muted. In fact, he's singing so softly that if I didn't see his beak and body move, I'd swear the song must be coming from somewhere far off on the hillside.

A flock of robins paused on its way south earlier this week. Alighting in the meadow across the road, the birds began to run over the ground in the way that robins do. Then, from the top of a tree on the hillside, came the

sound of May and apple blossoms and burgeoning life—
the familiar robin's carol. It was wispy, though, and hesitant, as if the songster needed to apologize for his remi-
niscence.

We can watch the "summer re-runs," as Peg calls them,
at our bird feeder. We keep the feeder going all year
round. In this way we attract some of the birds pictured
so confidently on the birdseed bags: orioles, catbirds,
rose-breasted grosbeaks, thrushes. We get a host of transients, too, during the fall migration. Encouraged by the
presence of the seed-and-suet-crowd, they linger around
the edges—myrtle warblers, yellow-breasted chats, field
sparrows, ruby-crowned kinglets. Although they've been
virtually silent for a month, they now sing little snatches
of song as if trying to recall those buoyant summer days.

I recall, too, a group of homesick starlings. It was well
past nesting time when I saw them—early October, in
fact. The starlings were most likely the ones that had occupied a hollow stub in our maple during the breeding
season. They landed in the tamarack tree near the hollow
old maple. Then one of them, apparently the mother, flew
repeatedly to the hole and looked inside. The other two,
doubtless the remnant of the original trio she'd raised,
dutifully streamed back and forth after her, sharing her
activity if not her excitement. After all, they could hardly
be expected to recall the stub. They'd seen it mainly from
the inside.

This performance continued for six or eight sorties between maple and tamarack. Then, after one last look, the
three of them flew off down the valley.

It was a simple case of bird behavior, I suppose. But it
looked as if the family was checking the old home place
before closing up and departing for the winter. Or so it
seemed to me.

The flaming colors of the foliage around those starlings bade farewell to summer too, of course. Unable to move to a more sheltered climate like the birds, the trees and shrubs have adopted the familiar practice of shedding those worn-out leaves. A marvelous device aids them in their task. By means of an ingenious arrangement a large elm or maple may drop as many as one million leaves in a short time without damage.

The secret of the shedding of the leaves—and, to a large extent, the secret of their autumn coloration as well —lies in a tiny ring of tissue at the base of each leaf. This ring, the abscission layer, is the point at which the leaf will break away from the twig. The abscission layer is composed of fragile, thin-walled cells. When the leaves are nearing the end of their useful life, the cells of the ring begin to develop. As they grow they interfere with the flow of materials in and out of the petiole, or leaf stalk. The familiar green of chlorophyll fades away.

Now the underlying colors show themselves. All season they have been masked by the intense green of chlorophyll, but they are slower to disappear as the leaf nears the end of its life. Hence they now become dominant: the yellow of xanthophyll and the orange of carotene. These two organic chemicals, vital to plant life, are normal components of the leaf cells. Why they are colored as they are is largely unknown.

This whole series of events is triggered, apparently, by our old friend the waning sun and its shortening days, rather than by some legendary Jack Frost with icy fingers. And as the chemistry of the leaf continues to change, the colors run the gamut: sunny yellow and crimson in the maples, the vermilion of woodbine, the purples of ash and oak, the bronze of the beeches.

The abscission layer completes its growth. Now the leaf

is joined to the twig by a few brittle cells. Then, one day, a playful gust of wind wrenches it free.

More dramatically, one of those calm cold nights brings a frost that permeates the abscission cells, rupturing them with tiny ice crystals. Then come the rays of the warming sun, melting the crystals. As the final tether is loosed, the leaf drops—often in company with hundreds of others, released at that very second. I have stood under a tree on a frosty morning and seen nearly the entire mass of leaves cascade around me in a fluttering, whispering shower as the sun rose.

The sugar maples and the beeches—and especially the oaks—seem reluctant to part with the last of their foliage. A few of the seemingly fragile leaves may cling, withered and brown, for the entire winter. Woodsmen tell of a condemned logger who, when allowed one last request, asked that he not be executed until the oak in the prison yard had lost all its leaves—which, in all likelihood, would be never.

There are lingering farewells on the forest floor as well as in the canopy above. Protected from early frosts, the creatures of the tree roots and rotting vegetation find their lives gradually slowing to the long pause of winter. And among the more vocal of the goodbyes is that sung by the spring peeper. I have heard him right up into December. If there is any creature that seems to hate to quit, it's this diminutive tree frog.

You might think that the peeper, cold-blooded as it is, would find little point in staying up beyond the golden days of September. But apparently even a few hours of sunshine on a November day are enough incentive. Although it's small enough to sit on your thumbnail with hardly anything hanging over, the spring peeper makes up in enthusiasm for what it lacks in size.

Prodded into activity by a balmy late-autumn day, the blithe peeper hops out from under a rotting log. Inflating the resonance pouch beneath its throat with every note, it emits a few encouraging peeps at the waning sun. These are scarcely the familiar lusty yelps of mating time in the spring swamps but they're a heartening sound, even if they're half a year out of season.

One of the best places to see this little frog is on a country road on a rainy autumn night. Your headlights may pick out the gleam of its white underside as it sits up straight in the rain. It looks like a pebble glistening on the asphalt. The "pebble" may crouch as your car approaches, or it may take off in long leaps to the other side of the road, three feet at a jump.

There are other frogs on that rainy road: wood frogs, leopard frogs, pickerel frogs,. There are toads and salamanders, too, and a conglomeration of other creatures—earthworms, snails, slugs, millipedes. There seem to be more, proportionally, than in summer when life was abundant everywhere.

There's a good reason for this convocation in the dark. A thermometer would quickly tell you why. The massive ribbon of pavement retains the heat of the day and releases it slowly through the night. Those autumn stay-awakes, out for one last jaunt, come upon the cozy surface of this great, flat stove. They linger a while, and as the night wears on the population grows. A census of the strollers along this gigantic boulevard might include almost any of the small creatures that have not yet turned in for the winter. Even a cottontail rabbit pauses now and again and sits down to warm himself.

Since the surface also acts as a radiator for the air above it, you will see small moths of several species, collectively called "fall millers" by my Vermont neighbors. These inch-long aerialists will keep extending the season as long as possible. Bats, attracted by the warmth and the easy hunting above the roadway, course up and down in a regular beat. They'll soon be going into hibernation, but for these remaining nights they'll enjoy good hunting in the evening of their year.

It was a chance meeting with one of these lingering creatures that started my career as a naturalist. One Thanksgiving Day I wanted to help my mother with the dinner so the turkey wouldn't take so long. She assured me that I could help her most by taking a walk with my father.

The weather had been warm the day before, but it had cooled during the night. There were a few snowflakes in the air. As we kicked our way through the leaves, I uncovered something strange. It was a baby wood turtle— stiff and cold, but still alive. It was lying at the edge of the road, scarcely covered by the leaves. We couldn't imagine why it should be abroad on such a chilly day. I slipped it into my pocket to take back and show my mother.

Dad suggested that I write to the naturalist, Thornton Burgess, inquiring what faulty time schedule had brought a little turtle out to freeze. I never thought I'd get an answer, but in a couple of weeks a letter came in the mail. The biographer of Peter Rabbit assured me that the turtle had probably been wandering on the warm road the previous afternoon and had stayed too long before trying to find shelter. "If you hadn't come along to rescue him," the letter said, "the turtle surely would have perished."

The letter, two pages long, was typewritten, single-spaced, and signed, "Your friend, Thornton Burgess." There and then I decided that if one of the attributes of a naturalist was to take such pains with the query of a seven-

year-old boy, I'd be a naturalist, too. I've never fal-
tered in that resolve—although the turtle, alas, died from
exposure a few days later.

Turtles and frogs and their cold-blooded companions
bid goodbye to the fading year, for the most part, in silence. The chorus of crickets and grasshoppers is a thing
of the past, too, but there are still a few survivors of
their grassblade legions. We admire their hardiness as
they struggle back in dwindling numbers after every
frost. But we hadn't realized just how courageous they
could be until that autumn of 1969.

The first part of October gave no hint of what was
coming. Daytime temperatures averaged nearly seventy
degrees. The golden sun filtered down through the remaining autumn foliage. Then on the twenty-first of the
month it began to rain. The temperature started to drop.
By the morning of October 22 the rain had turned to snow.
By noon we had nearly half a foot of the wet, sticky stuff.
It covered the yet-green lawns and settled on wire fences
so they looked like ropes. It clung to still-leafy branches
until they crashed to earth with its weight.

Still the snow came. It fell all afternoon and most of
the night. In the morning when it finally stopped, we
took a yardstick and gauged its depth out on our south
meadow. Eleven to fourteen inches. Counting what had
melted into the ground, there must have been nearly a
foot and a half of snow. A radio report from the Burlington weather station indicated this was a record snowfall.

By dusk the temperature had dropped to twenty degrees. And the next morning we could scarcely believe
the thermometer: it registered a startling ten degrees
above zero.

The snow stayed for ten days. Then the weather turned
mild again. The warm sun melted the snow until our

river ran swollen as if with a spring thaw. Peg and I took a walk on the meadow across the road. We detoured around the few remaining patches of snow, making our way up the hillside.

As we neared a jumble of tall meadow grass, a familiar note came to me on the breeze. It was the summer sound of a grasshopper.

So the cold hadn't killed them all. We turned our heads this way and that, trying to locate the sound. For several moments the whisper of rustling grass thwarted us, but at last the breeze died down. And at once the whereabouts of the grasshopper became apparent. He was right at our feet, swaying at the top of a brown spike of timothy. Scraping legs against wings in an intermittent buzzing sound, he was making his last stand.

His note was only an echo of the confident *psst-psst-psst* of a month ago, but it was a grasshopper's song, nonetheless. We listened intently, hoping to hear another singing male, but there was none. Since the female grass-hopper usually dies soon after laying her eggs, he was probably singing to no ears but ours. And so the three of us stood there in our tiny patch of summer, with a winter snowbank only eight feet away.

Although the forlorn green grasshopper was apparently the sole survivor of its kind on that early November day, there were other insects soaking up the last bit of sun-light. A dozen gnats danced up and down above a clump of whitened goldenrod. Several caddis flies fluttered up from the undergrowth as we walked along. They quickly dropped to earth again, to fold their brown wings, tent-like, over their bodies. Then each one turned so that it would be broadside to the warmth of the sun.

While we watched the caddis flies, there was a rustling

in the leaves at the base of an alder. Poking along in the sunshine was a black ground beetle. It was hunting for a caterpillar just as a late bird hunts for a later worm. And as we were about to cross the bridge back to our own lawn, a sulphur butterfly danced in front of us. It reminded me of a midnight reveler on one last round. It found what it wanted, too: a single wild mustard plant, raising a dozen yellow four-petaled blossoms in defiance of the coming winter.

The butterfly paused, then skipped away. But in pinpointing that wild mustard plant it reminded us of other blooms that struggle along until they are so frozen that they can survive no more. Along the road to town, for instance, a single chickory plant bravely raised those blue blossoms until November, even though the roadside was brown and dead. Buttercups bloomed in our backyard all through October, and every year or two hardy dandelions stubbornly keep going until the snow finally covers them.

In front of our house there is a clump of old-fashioned farmyard asters. I've taken photographs of their purple blooms borne four feet above the snow on sturdy stalks. So bravely do they cling to life that it's hard to tell when they've finally given up. Their flowers gradually become brittle and get progressively darker in the autumn storms; we say they're turning black and blue. Sometimes we've gathered a handful of them for a Thanksgiving centerpiece. It takes a little imagination to call them an attractive bouquet, but at least they're fresh-picked.

The whole point, of course, is that if you depended on the living things to tell you what season it was, you might be way off the mark. Try to find a groundhog or woodchuck now, for instance, and you discover that he may have turned in for the winter as early as September. It seems that when the living is easiest—food in abundance, warm sunny days that hover in the eighties—that's when he often elects to start his winter nap.

Or, since procrastinators are the creatures at hand here, there are a few animals that are just now getting around to that all-absorbing activity of life: the reproduction of the species. The porcupine is one of our woodland neighbors that turns its efforts to this task. Nearsighted to a fault, and able to distinguish only shadows more than half a dozen feet away, the porcupine relies on other than visual means to find members of the opposite sex.

One of these methods is to snuff along the ground or up a likely tree trunk with that sensitive nose. Porcupines have a distinctive aroma, not unlike the combination of smells from a fruit stand, with a strong emphasis on the pineapple. It's not unpleasant, and quite apart from the smell of a porpcupine den. Such a cave or hollow log will get highly noisome in winter after it's been occupied by a few of the quill pigs, temporarily snowbound by a blizzard.

A surer means, considering the slowness with which the porcupine travels when the going is good—about as fast as a person's leisurely stroll—is to utilize its keen sense of hearing. A porcupine can hear a whisper at thirty feet above all the other sounds of the countryside. We used to call our own pet porcupine, Piney, in such a fashion from his perch in our tall maple.

So the myopic porcupine shuffles through the woods in the fall, humming to himself in squeaky little grunts. His potential mate is doing the same thing. The meeting of the two precipitates a duet that has few equals in the animal world short of a couple of cats on a fence.

Seasoned woodsmen have clutched their rifles and stared apprehensively out into the dark beyond the fire during a porcupine serenade. Less experienced campers are apt to build the fire to a roaring blaze and keep it crackling all night to force those banshees—or whatever they are—to stay out of the circle of firelight. Yowls and wails alternate with cries of distress and plaintive little songs of endearment as those two porcupines plight their troth in the company of whatever witnesses there are to keep their distance.

And how do porcupines mate? Simple—and the answer is not "very carefully." They mate in the same fashion as other quadrupeds. It is only when the quills of a porky are erected in fear or rage that they become formidable weapons. Normally they lie harmless along the back and sides, protected and overlain by long, coarse guard hairs. Thus the porcupine seeks and safely wins the object of his fancy in the chilly late autumn.

A mated pair of porkies may stay together for a month or more. However, as several of them may den up in a ledge or rockfall during a storm, the ties between any two may get a little hazy. Monogamy is not necessarily the rule. If one female is sought by two males, there may be a bout of pushing and shoving, accompanied by wailing, teeth-chattering, and a few well-directed nips. Like the skunk, however, the porcupine saves its ultimate weapon for use only against strangers. Members of its own kind are relatively safe from those lethal spines. Besides, porcupines are good-natured animals and most arguments are settled amicably.

No porcupine, of course, throws its quills—at least intentionally. The spines are loosely attached to the skin by a slender base. The fifteen pound rodent, lashing out with its quill-studded tail, may whack against a solid object and shake one or two of them loose. The quills travel only a few feet, however, and rattle harmlessly to earth. The porky cannot shoot its spines at a foe any more than other mammals can throw their hair. In fact, the quills of a porcupine *are* hairs—thirty thousand of them on a full-grown specimen. Like hairs, also, they can be replaced when lost.

One more question about porcupines. Granted that those quills, when lying passively along the body, are no threat to the mating process, the next point concerns the young. Are they born essentially naked and defenseless—like mice, for instance, or bear cubs—or do they have quills from birth? And if they do begin life fully armed, how can such a prickly baby be born without hurting the mother?

Actually, the young porcupette, as it is called, will be brought into the world next spring in the natural, normal way. It is clothed in spines, yes, but these are overlain with a covering of silky hair. Besides, the spines, although well-formed, are soft and moist. Only when they dry in air do they become hardened—about as stiff as the central shaft of a bird's wing feather. In addition, the porcupine is born while still encased in its fetal membranes, like a newborn puppy or kitten. So there is no danger to the female during birth.

Helped out of the membrane by its mother, the young porcupine erects those spines a few times to facilitate drying. Then, almost at once, it ambles along after her through the March and April woodlands. Now it is a self-sufficient, one-pound porcupine—ready to climb, to sample tender new leaves and its mother's milk, and to shuffle amiably through a respectful world.

By late fall the porcupine's graceful neighbor, the deer, has polished those new antlers and bears them noiselessly through the bushes and trees as he seeks his mate. Apparently he uses his adornments only against his own rivals, relying on his speed and sharp hoofs as protection against other creatures. But his antlers often prove his undoing. They can become tangled with his foe so the two animals remain locked together until they starve.

Members of the deer family may transfer their pugnacity to non-deer neighbors—even, sometimes, to humans. Every autumn or two someone gets chased out of the Vermont woods by a vindictive buck. A farmer near Montpelier went out to call his cows one frosty morning —and was startled to see the whole herd bearing down on him at full speed. As it thundered closer he saw it was spearheaded by a four-point buck with blood in its eye.

The farmer shouted and the deer came to its senses. Shaking those antlers in defiance, it bounded off through the pasture. But the cows, nostrils flaring, veered away from the barn. Only after suitable prancing and snorting and coquettish arching of necks did the buck's would-be harem subside into Holsteins once more.

It's not rare, either, for bucks to "test" the males of other species when the chance affords. We saw this take place one memorable autumn morning on our north meadow. We'll not soon forget the meeting between a fully-antlered buck and a Chincoteague pony who was feeling his oats.

The pony was an outsized souvenir of a trip to the tidewater town of Chincoteague, Virginia. He was one of approximately two hundred ponies that roam the island of Assateague, just offshore of Chincoteague. These animals, descendents of ponies that were probably shipwrecked there years ago, find a living on the salt marshes among the fiddler crabs and mosquitoes.

It's a tough life and the sparse vegetation will support only just so many of the hardy little horses. So every year in July the wild ponies are herded together and driven into the water between Assateague and Chincoteague. They swim the channel—stallions, mares, colts and all—to a corral where the young-of-the-year are separated out and sold at auction.

I had an assignment to do a story on "Pony Penning," as it is called, so Peg and I took two of our children along to see the auction. And, auctions being what they are, we'd purchased one of the colts in a moment of weakness. We named him "Little Fellow," piled him into our van-type station wagon along with Roger and Alison, and drove the whole affair back to our hundred acres in Vermont.

Now, four months later, Little Fellow was grazing in the late autumn mists with our two mares and Yankee, our big gelding. They nosed through the dying goldenrod and the fading blue of the asters, seeking the last wisps of grass in the overgrown pasture. Suddenly, from the edge of the woods, a buck deer leaped the fence and came bounding to within fifty yards of the four horses. Snorting, he slid to a stiff-legged stop and lowered his antlers in challenge.

Yankee and the mares just looked at him. Little Fellow, however, rose to the situation. The other three horses always seemed too dignified to frolic with a six-month-old colt, but this was a chance to play. Tail raised and head high, he galloped forward.

We watched, not knowing what would happen. Although Little Fellow's three hundred pounds was about double that of the buck, he scarcely had the maneuverability of a deer. If that buck really wanted trouble, our Chincoteague pony might be in for a surprise.

We needn't have worried. Youth wins friends almost anywhere, and Little Fellow's manner said "play" rather than "fight." The buck's attitude changed at once. Wheeling, he raced in a great circle of the pasture, with the pony in full pursuit. Then, at some signal, the game reversed and the two came leaping back toward Yankee and the mares.

Now they all entered the game. First one would be "it" and then another. For perhaps five minutes they raced through the pasture in a spirited game of tag. We watched, enthralled, as a wild creature laid aside the fear of man and everything associated with him, and abandoned itself to a joyous romp.

Then, suddenly, the game was over. The buck vaulted the fence. He watched for a moment to see if the horses would follow. Then, raising his white tail, he was gone.

The deer's impressive cousin, the moose, can become a menace in these days of the autumn rut. A biologist friend of mine had a close call as he was doing some autumn studies on this largest member of the deer family. In following the tracks of a bull moose he suddenly discovered he'd gone in a big circle. This meant his quarry could well be behind him instead of vice versa.

"The minute I realized what was going on," my friend told me, "I headed for the nearest tree to reconnoiter. And it's lucky I did. That bull moose came out of a thicket like a locomotive. I got to the tree about twenty feet ahead of him."

In my friend's haste, the lens cap of his camera went clattering to the ground. It was a lucky turn of events, for it served as a focal point for the bull's rage. After he'd demolished the lens cap and driven it into the soil with those massive hoofs, he turned and strode away without a backward glance. Otherwise my friend might have spent half the day in that tree.

A few of the smaller mammals have their last fling on these crisp autumn days, as well. Our common little brown bat follows the lead set earlier by his larger cousin, the red bat. He may overtake his half-ounce mate in the early evening air, or he may discover her in the condominium of a cave, where hundreds of his species of both sexes gather for their daily sleep. And in some rocky cave or abandoned mole burrow, the long-tailed weasel may still be seeking a musky-smelling mate, as his breeding season extends from late summer into fall.

It's somewhat of a concession when weasels mate. With the exception of the otter, most members of the weasel family are solitary—and militantly so. They are apt to fight if they chance to meet. While a skunk or a midwestern badger may be seen in the company of others of its kind, these are usually the young of the year. Mink and weasel males may help in gathering food for the family, but as soon as the young are self-sufficient, they all become loners—just like their wilderness cousins, the marten, the fisher, and the wolverine.

Aquatic life also bids its farewell to the season. Although many residents of ponds and streams mated in spring and summer, a few fish lay their eggs in the autumn waters. The brook trout in our river are active now, for instance. We can see specimens of both sexes, resplendent in many hues, their orange fins bordered with white as they wend steadily upstream to the smaller brooks. There the female will lie on her side, her tail patting out a spot in the gravel for the eggs. The male will follow her every move, fertilizing the tapioca-sized eggs with copious milt in the swift cold water. Lake trout breed in the shallows now, as do the whitefishes of the Great Lakes.

So, whether they fly or crawl or swim, the performers continue to act out their lives. And the prize for perseverance among all of them could well go to that tireless worker, the honeybee.

It has taken momentous effort on the part of the bees to produce the honey needed to carry the hive through the winter. Each pound of the sweet represents the nectar brought from more than fifty thousand trips afield. If all the mileage flown by the bees for that one pound were somehow put together, it would reach twice around the earth—some fifty thousand miles. Or, looked at in another way, the distance necessary to travel for ten pounds of honey is equal to a round trip to the moon. And there may be more than a hundred pounds of honey in a good-sized hive.

Such production is a constant drain on the resources of the hive and its workers. The single queen performs as an egg-laying machine, producing new offspring at the rate of one every thirty seconds—more than two thousand a day. After nearly three weeks as a grub in a waxen cradle, each new bee takes its place among the work force in the hive.

For a few days the newly-transformed bee cleans the hive and cares for her younger sisters. Then she embarks on the final stage of her career, the gathering of nectar from the flowers. Bees hatched late in the season seek this nectar as long as the weather will permit. Thus, when the last rose of summer finally blooms each year, there's probably a bee to visit it.

So hard does the bee work that her total productive life may last only a month. As she reaches that early old age, her wings become frayed and discolored. They have to beat harder to carry her loads of pollen and nectar to the hive.

Busy to the last, the honeybee has to forage farther as the flowers die in autumn. On a summer day she may visit a thousand blossoms; now she'll be lucky to find fifty. Finally the time comes when she can no longer fly back to the hive. The tired old wings can support her no more.

She launches out into the air from that last flower, staggers a few yards, and descends to earth. Climbing another stalk, she tries again. Bit by bit, she draws closer to home. If there are no convenient stalks to climb, she simply walks—or, rather, runs with buzzing wings—in the direction of that unseen hive. It must be a wearying journey, over sticks and stones and clumps of grass. At last, on some return voyage, she can go no farther.

Her lifeless body is eventually found by a shrew or mouse, which bears it home to feed to its latest litter. Thus the bee remains useful, even in death.

Her valiant effort, in a way, typifies the struggle of all living things. The very fact of existence carries with it the obligation to continue.

On they go, as they always have. A lone grasshopper creaks out a scratchy goodbye from a sunny hillside. A spring peeper pipes a few last notes among the falling leaves. A late-blooming aster braces up against a November gale, and a sapsucker reminisces at the edge of an old barn.

Actually, we enjoy the sapsucker even if he does shatter our eardrums. It's a bittersweet time of the year, and it's good to know that others are going to miss summer, too. So, let him rattle on the roof.

Besides, maybe next year he'll hammer out his dawn farewell at noon.

7

Winter Warning

THE first snow of the season began at dusk. It fell all night in wet, sticky flakes that clung where they landed. Peg and I took a walk in the morning through the silent wonderland. We marveled at the cottony puffs that rested on the remaining yellow leaves of the poplars. We exclaimed over the forks of the limbs, so brimful of snow that we couldn't tell where the branches joined. And we stood dumbfounded as we came to a trail that led from yesterday's autumn into today's winter.

The trail was a trail of blood.

We bent for a moment, scrutinizing the double line of webbed footprints, the thin drag mark of a tail. A muskrat, and a small one, from the looks. It had come up from the river bank and had made its way across the snowy lawn toward the corner of the house.

We followed the path with our eyes. It ended beneath the syringa bush. And there was the muskrat. He had gone as far as his strength would allow. Now he huddled beneath the bush, his face bitten and his nose almost gone.

We tried to piece the story together. The gravelly bank of our river supports a rather sparse vegetation along its steep sides: sedges, a few shrubs, a handful of struggling cattails. These have barely maintained a muskrat family for years, with little forage left over for grown youngsters. Ordinarily the young go poking along the shore in August and September to find their own patch of edible plants, but this little fellow had been different. He had probably refused to leave at the appointed time.

His parents may have grudgingly accepted his presence through those warm autumn days. But when four inches of snow covered nearly everything edible along that scanty riverbank, the picture changed. With raw survival at stake, the old muskrats turned on the youngster. One must perish or all would perish. And the end result of the family squabble was a brown furry object, the size of a small cat, huddled in misery beneath the syringa bush.

We threw an old coat over the wounded animal, then carefully unfolded it to where we could look at him. His nose would never be the same, but he'd survive. We put him in a large cage with a dishpan of water so he could keep his skin wet, and fed him apples and vegetables for a few days. That weekend we released him in a nearby swamp where the competition wasn't so keen.

Soon the snow would melt and the ground would be bare. Winter was yet an official six weeks away. But the muskrats hadn't been able to wait. All freeloaders had to go—even if it had involved ousting their own flesh and blood from the family den.

Our explorations that snowy morning also brought us to an empty vireo's nest in a small maple tree. It was just above eye level, so we stepped close to examine the soft grasses and plant fibers showing beneath the rounded dome of snow that covered it. As I pulled the twig down for a better look, the nest quivered violently. The snow fell away, revealing that the nest wasn't as empty as we had figured. It was roofed over with leaves and grass. One side of the roof was incomplete, and from the resulting gap peered the inquisitive eyes of a white-footed mouse. Its nose twinkled as it sampled the air for clues as to what had tilted its home so crazily.

This mouse had made its stand for the winter. Others like it invade our farmhouse each autumn, finally digging in after they have checked all possibilities for shelter. Doubtless this whitefoot had stores of seeds in a few hidden crannies. Much of its winter would be spent in the refurbished vireo's nest, with occasional jaunts to the secret pantry. Indeed, when I went to close up the little cabin where our guests sometimes spend the night, I found what may have been the whitefoot's choicest larder. This was a plastic bag in a bureau on the back porch. The bag had held several pairs of nylon stockings. Now the stockings had been hauled away and were replaced by wild cherry pits.

Those storehouses of mice also serve as supplements to the diets of squirrels, other mice and, occasionally, sharp-eyed blue jays. A few weeks earlier in the season their woodland caches could have been raided by their huge neighbor, the black bear, in hopes of finding a store of beechnuts or dried berries.

At the brink of winter, however, the bear's search is of a different nature. He will soon den up beneath a ledge or under the roots of a dead tree, but he has a task to accomplish first. And that task is to fill his capacious innards with just the right mixture of twigs, grasses, and pine needles.

These inedibles form a series of plugs that remain almost stationary during the bear's winter sleep. Apparently they keep the digestive tract open and in good condition, ready for the ants, grubs, fruit, small mammals, roots, and berries that are standard fare the rest of the year. And so, now that the long-term preparation of a layer of fat has been accomplished, the bear sets itself for the winter ahead by grazing beneath the pines and among the grass clumps like a portly, short-legged cow.

Although, in the minds of many people, the bear hibernates in winter, its retreat during the cold months is more in the form of a prolonged nap. A truly hibernating mammal such as a chipmunk seems near to death. Its body temperature has dropped to within a few degrees of the chilly soil that surrounds it. Breathing is so shallow and infrequent that no movement can be seen; the feeble respiration does not even fog a mirror placed in front of the rodent's nose. The heartbeat slows to a few pulses each minute—a far cry from the throbbing two hundred or more beats per minute of the active chipmunk chattering on a woodland stump. Indeed, the blood flows so slowly that a cut will not even bleed.

The sleeping bear, on the other hand, maintains its vital functions almost at normal. Its breathing is slow and measured, as with any animal in profound slumber. Its pulse rate has slowed somewhat, but still averages about once a second, depending on sex and age of the bear. The sleeping mammal maintains its body temperature within a few degrees of normal, but is so well insulated by its winter coat that snow drifting in at the mouth of its cave filters down on that thick fur without melting.

One of the unforgettable experiences of a friend happened when he was cross-country skiing in the woods a few miles from our house. He noticed an odd snowdrift beneath the base of an uprooted tree. The surface of the drift was honeycombed with peculiar, almost hexagonal, patches of snow. Curious, he poked his ski pole at the largest patch, about six inches in diameter.

At once the cracks between all the patches widened. One edge of the snowdrift crumbled away, revealing a clump of heavy black moss. Then, to my friend's astonishment, the "moss" blinked and turned in his general direction.

That was all the information my friend needed. The strange snowdrift, it turned out, was the body of a slumbering bear. The snow had assumed the honeycomb texture because of the slight bit of warmth that penetrated through the fur. And, when the bear had been prodded, its involuntary intake of breath caused the patches to separate from each other.

Although the black bear normally shuns contact with humans, there was no telling what this creature would do when it found itself face to face with an intruder. The question remains unanswered, however. Befogged by sleep, the bear's bleary eyes failed to discern the skiier, who stood as though rooted to the spot. Its keen sense of smell failed to pick out any unusual scent, either. The animal returned to its nap while my friend, who said his heart was pounding so hard he was sure it would wake the bear again, waited five minutes before setting a new woodland cross-country ski record.

The animals that remain active all year are making final preparations, too. The weasel gradually sheds his golden-brown coat. All except the dark tail tip is replaced hair for hair by winter's white. Then the lithe creature, practically indistinguishable from its Old World ermine cousins, can pursue mice and rabbits, its leaping form all but invisible save for the shadow it casts on the snow.

The snowshoe hare also changes from summer brown to winter white—except for the dark tips of those long ears. Hence it is often called the varying hare. The change is a gradual one, roughly matching the slow whitening of the landscape.

Sometimes the hare gets out of synchronization with its surroundings. The weather is not as predictable as the steadily shortening days that tell the hare when the time for its transformation has arrived. An early snowstorm may catch it in the act of changing color, so that it is neither brown nor white, but speckled. And during an open winter when the ground remains bare, the snow-white creature may be stranded in a brown landscape, fair game for predators.

The color change in mammals is an intricate process, still not completely understood, but it involves the amount of light falling on the eye. As the days shorten, the lessening degree of optic stimulation affects a tiny gland hidden deep within the head. This gland, the pituitary, is called the "master gland" because it affects so many of the other glands of the body.

Even in humans, the pituitary is only the size of a pea. In a small forest animal it may be no larger than a match head. Tiny as it is, however, the pituitary produces a number of powerful hormones. These enter the bloodstream and are transported throughout the body. In animals that change color, the hormones trigger other glands which, in turn, regulate the shedding of the brown summer hair and the growth of white winter hair to replace it.

The same shift in hormones causes another change in the snowshoe hare. A thick mat of fur develops in the space between and around the toes, especially the hind feet. Thus the hare lives up to its name, with "snowshoes" that may propel the tomcat-sized body eight or ten feet at a bound over the soft snow. Since it seldom seeks shelter other than beneath an overhanging evergreen, the snowshoe hare might be said to trust in a lucky rabbit's foot—indeed, four of them.

A lesser color change takes place in our white-tailed deer. Partly camouflaged in summer with a red-brown, almost rusty, color allowing it to blend with the dry leaves of the forest floor, the deer takes on a pepper-and-salt gray to match the frosty landscape. Its fur is denser than in summer, too, as are the coats of most of its neighbors. They become glossy and luxuriant, often so thick that they cannot be parted down to the skin.

Such a thick pelt is a marvelous protection against winter's chill. But it may also bring with it the kiss of death. For the rich coat of an animal in winter pelage is referred to as "prime" by furriers. And thus begins the deadly winter game—the mink and muskrat and beaver and fox going about, all unknowing, in those magnificent coats while a million trappers endeavor to take the coats away and place them on someone they do not even know.

Tree squirrels also dress for winter, but there is such a premium on agility in the treetops that a heavy pelt would be a drawback. A little fur is added, but the most noticeable change is apt to be in the tail. It may increase to half again its diameter.

This bushy appendage has a special importance in the case of the little aerialist. Like a rudder, it keeps the tree squirrel on course during its dizzying leaps. It also serves somewhat the same function as a bullfighter's cape: a cornered squirrel will whisk that tail in the opposite direction to which it moves, confounding its enemy. And, when the winter air snaps with the cold, the squirrel covers its nose with that fluffy comforter as it beds down to sleep.

My Vermont neighbors pay more than passing attention to a squirrel's tail as winter approaches. It is one means whereby they try to predict the coming season. If the tail looks about as it did during the summer, a mild winter is in the offing. But if it's handsome and thick and nearly as big as its owner, look out: there's a long, cold winter ahead.

The country dweller scrutinizes all manner of signs in an attempt to forecast the winter to come. Along with the condition of the pelts of animals, there is their protective layer of fat. The thicker the fat, the more dramatic the prediction. Lots of fat means a hard winter.

The activity of animals and fish is important, too. If the fishing drops off markedly, it means the fish have left the shallows and retreated to deeper water while there is yet time. An unusual number of dead snakes in the road means they're headed for their dens—another portentous sign. Heavy crops of fruit signal a hard winter, too. And if the bears and chipmunks and woodchucks drop out of sight earlier than usual, it means they probably know something that we don't.

The most famous weather prophet, however, is the woolly bear caterpillar. This larva of the common whitish Isabella moth sports a bristly crew-cut arranged in three bands: black head and forepart, rusty-brown middle, and black tail section. According to my neighbors, the three portions forecast the beginning, middle, and end of winter.

Many caterpillar viewers say that a wide, brown middle means a mild winter with plenty of brown grass and leaves. An abbreviated black forward section means win-

ter will start with a vengeance. And watch out for a caterpillar whose black nether section begins around the
middle and continues unabated to the rear of his hurrying little body. This means winter will drag on and on as
if it would never end.

Other specialists come up with different readings. A
broad center section, they say, means deep snow—a real
old-fashioned winter, rather than a mild open one. Lots of
black on the tail section, rather than signifying that winter will last forever, indicates an early spring. So you take
your choice. Quite understandably, at the end of every
winter, there's some caterpillar connoisseur who can
smile and say, "I told you so."

And how does the expert—the woolly bear—live up to
its own predictions? It simply refuses to enter into the ar-
gument at all. Hurrying across the road and into a pile of
leaves, it curls up for the winter and goes fast asleep.

Other caterpillars tell of the impending season in their
own ways. Several species will spend the winter in their
present state, like the woolly bear, rather than transform-
ing into adults before the cold arrives. These kinds have
chewed their way through the greenery as long as it
lasted. Now, with little food left, they appear on the sides
of buildings, the bark of trees, on bulldozers and baby
carriages. Looking for winter shelter, they spread their
kind over lawns and gardens and parking lots. There they
are carried still further by cars, trucks, and even air-
planes.

Cluster flies—those insects that visited the skunk cab-
bages last spring—make their appearance again. Like the
caterpillars, they have been active all along, but now that
winter is actually at hand, they gather by the thousands.
They are joined by ladybird beetles, whose diet of aphids
has failed. Along with box elder bugs and elm leaf beetles

they heed the general call to quarters, as it were, on the inside of your windows.

The urge to congregate is more than some hazy desire for sociability in these insects. It is a definite need for as much bodily contact as possible. Known to scientists as positive thigmotropism, this tendency leads the insects to seek any potential avenue to shelter: the space between clapboards on a house, the gap around the edge of a loose-fitting window, even the keyhole in a door.

In these beetles and flies, thigmotropism is generally positive when the temperature is falling, thus leading numbers of them to crowd into the smallest possible space. In huddling together they keep slightly active, thus warming themselves a bit by muscular movement.

When the temperature rises, the reaction is reversed. Negative thigmotropism causes the insects to seek escape from the huddle. Emerging into a room, they are attracted to the light at the window. Their unheralded appearance brings dismay to the homeowner, who finds himself apparently invaded by some kind of plague.

The coming winter also affects the lives of the bees and wasps and hornets. They, too, must face the reality that cold will soon be upon them. Males are no longer needed, now that the new queens have been fertilized. So the honeybee drones are dragged outside the hive and dumped on their own. They fly back, only to be repulsed again and again. Wasp and hornet drones may be stung to death. The helpless larvae in their cells often meet the same swift fate—or find themselves abandoned by the workers who seem to have lost all purpose in life.

While the beehive maintains itself through the winter, its occupants nourished by their store of honey, the paper cities of the wasps and hornets become ghost towns. Often the late sunshine of a day in November or December will disclose a solitary queen wasp, investigating the holes and cracks along the side of a house. Carrying within herself the germ of next year's colony, she crawls deep into a crevice. There she remains through the winter, sometimes grasping a piece of wood in her jaws. By having this bit of wood ready and waiting next spring, she may thus give herself the necessary reminder as to what task needs doing: the chewing of wood into paper for her new home.

An undesired plum may fall to us following an insect's search for winter quarters. The female *Anopheles* mosquito—northern cousin of the vector of malaria in warmer climates—is with us all summer, an unbidden guest at picnics and beach parties. Now, as her human benefactors retire, she follows suit. She seeks the shelter of caves and ledges and hollow trees. You may find her, if you look, on the wall in a basement or lavatory, or in a kitchen cabinet.

From this vantage point, when the occasion offers, she may sally forth to attack. Once I noted one of these intrepid insects on the wall of an elevator in mid-Manhattan. She rode with me for two dozen floors, then continued on her way as I departed.

Many mosquitoes retire for the winter as adults, like *Anopheles*. Others, although they themselves may die, leave a legacy of aquatic larvae or floating rafts of eggs. Along with many other swimming insects—as well as pupae in the soil and grubs in rotting logs—the inert little bodies may be buried deep in a crystalline mass of ice without themselves freezing.

A jumping spider, having run out of insect prey, seeks a sheltered spot beneath an old board or stone. It makes a round mattress of silk, slightly smaller in diameter than a dime. It fashions a coverlet of more silk and binds the two halves together into a flattened bag. There, in its self-imposed prison, the spider awaits the subzero cold. The thin woven cocoon is so dense and tough that it is almost impossible to tear with the fingers without crushing its occupant. Probably its main purpose is to prevent the spider from becoming dehydrated, for even such a durable sleeping bag must afford little real warmth during those long winter days.

As a boy I used to marvel that such fragile creatures could endure those months of violence on the part of the weather. An entomology course in college helped me with the answer. It seems that water will freeze, yes; but water is not what flows in those little motes of life. The fluid of their bodies is a "soup" of many minerals and carbon compounds. As the days get chilly the soup becomes concentrated. A syrupy-sweet alcohol, known as glycerol, begins to accumulate. Glycerol is a fine antifreeze—related to the stuff we put in auto radiators—and protects those spiders and flies and caterpillars in their chilly beds.

Once I read a statement by John Burroughs that wood borers in a frozen log were like vanilla ice cream. For years I thought he referred to their color and appearance. Then, when I learned about glycerol, I considered the great naturalist's words again.

The chance for personal observation offered itself one day when I was cutting wood for our fire. As I split a decaying chunk, two borers were exposed, lying in the galleries they had excavated in the wood. I tasted one of them; it *was* as sweet as ice cream. So was the second. They were downright delicious.

Those borers, so eagerly sought by bears and skunks and primitive people, are like vanilla ice cream—in every way. More so, too, in November than in October, as the glycerol builds up in their bodies. Buried in their log they

are getting ready for the deep freeze in their own efficient, unseen fashion.

Suffused with antifreeze and protected from dehydra-
tion of bitter winds by tough jackets of woven silk, moth
cocoons hang in the branches of trees and shrubs. Before
pupation, the caterpillar may have caught the edges of a
leaf together around itself as added protection. There the
leaf hangs after the rest of the foliage has dropped, conspicuous along with old bird and hornet nests. And we,
noticing them for the first time, realize that their appearance out of nowhere is, in itself, a sign of winter.

Often those nests and cocoons are first pointed out to
us by the returning winter birds. Coming back from the
deep woods, the birds pick over the veritable insect zoo
in abandoned nests. They give those cocoons a good
going-over, too, but seldom have much success. The cocoons are usually swung at the end of a flimsy twig where
it's impossible for a bird to get a good sound whack. But
the birds keep trying every few days—just in case.

The first winter bird to return to our feeder is the
chickadee. It arrives as early as September. Dishevelled
and furtive, it shows the effects of a summer spent evad-
ing woodland enemies and providing food for half a
dozen clamoring young. There is little of the confidence it
will show in a few weeks. It snatches a sunflower seed
and escapes with it to our big maple. There it hammers at
the seed, glancing around between pecks as if it expected
to flee at any moment.

At about the same time a large blue-white bird may
leave the shelter of the trees on the hill behind the house,
fly high over our valley, and disappear in the opposite
woods. The blue jay is scouting the area. It, too, shows
the effects of a summer spent protecting the young. So
carefully does it guard its nest of twigs that it may alight

in a nearby tree and stealthily climb up to the nest like a lizard. It will take weeks for the jay to regain its bird-feeder manners and become the blatant, screaming bully that makes you rue the day it found your feeder—even as you admire its natty colors and perky crest.

The striking black and yellow evening grosbeaks arrive from Canada sometime in October. In a few weeks they'll settle down to the feeder, shelling out sunflower seeds by the quart. Now, however, they'll content themselves with nipping buds and seeds in the tops of the trees. Juncos and white-throated sparrows come down from the higher reaches of Mt. Abraham. For them our Vermont valley is "south," even with its occasional thirty-below tempera-ture, and they'll stay until spring.

The real winter birds—tree sparrows, pine grosbeaks, and the striking snow buntings, who tuck their feet into their feathers and row themselves over the powdery drifts with their wings—seldom arrive before the first snow-flakes. And, every few years, the annual southern advance of the polar chill is preceded by the ghostly appearance of the great snowy owl. Suddenly materializing on a fencepost in a farmyard, the owl spreads consternation among the resident sparrows and pigeons.

Heralds of winter, these new arrivals—just as sure as the bluebird tells of spring. And to the bewildered birder there's another sign of the times: the appearance of those "Confusing Fall Warblers" pictured helpfully by Roger Tory Peterson in his celebrated *A Field Guide To The Birds*. These warblers are on their way south—the same vociferous host of blue and orange and fiery red that passed north in May. Now, having changed their plum-age, they are garbed in olive-drab and almost speechless, as befits a retreating army.

The most dramatic transformation may overtake one of

our largest upland birds during these weeks just before winter. The outward appearance of this bird hardly changes, but its behavior is sometimes so remarkably altered that the Amerindians used to call this time of year "The Crazy Moon" in its honor. And the crazy moon isn't always confined to the woods where the bird makes its home. Two years ago it came right into our house. Literally.

I was sitting in my upstairs study, pecking out the words to a magazine article on my clattering old Underwood No. 5. Our dog, Rebel, lay in his usual spot beneath the shelf that holds the biology books and government publications. His feet twitched in some exciting dream. Other than the two of us, there was nobody at home on that November afternoon.

Suddenly there was an explosion, attended by the sound of splintering glass. Rebel came to his feet, barking.

I ran down the stairs. There were pieces of glass halfway across the rug. The drapes fluttered at the edge of the bay window. And the window itself had a hole the size of a basketball.

Looking in the direction of the strewn glass, I saw an unfamiliar object over by the piano. As I watched, the object struggled to its feet. It was about the size and shape of a small chicken, and covered with feathers the color of the forest floor. Now I knew the cause of the explosion—a ruffed grouse, rocketing across our valley, had crashed headlong through the window.

Running for my camera, I managed to get a picture of our unusual visitor. Then, before I could pick up the grouse, it came to its senses, thundered off in full flight toward the window, and hit the glass with a thud.

I picked up the stricken bird. Its dark eyes gazed at me

for a moment, and it spread that magnificent tail, so like that of a little brown turkey. Then, throwing its head back, it died in my hands.

Why does the ruffed grouse go through this late-autumn madness? What causes an occasional cock-of-the-woods to abandon all caution and fly into the sides of buildings, the open window of a car, or even straight out to sea? Maybe it's some disease; a virus perhaps. Possibly it is caused by a parasite or an attack of some form of avian epilepsy. Some scientists think it may come from eating insects that have dined on an unwholesome mushroom. Still other theories range all the way from too many fermented frost grapes to a lack of some trace mineral in the diet. But the truth is still largely hidden, for the grouse is almost impossible to raise and study in the laboratory. And only one grouse in a dozen, perhaps, will show the malady.

At any rate, there was the grouse, whether you could explain it or not. This irrational behavior is all the more astonishing because it is in such contrast to the usual ways of the wily bird. When flushed by a hunter it veers around behind the nearest tree, putting the tree between itself and the danger. On a bitter winter night it will dive into a snowdrift, there to remain snug against the cold. And it's so clever at feigning a broken wing and crying piteously in pain that it can lure even an experienced old fox away from its chicks.

Those chicks, themselves, are gifted little creatures. Half the size of a domestic chick, they are hatched with all their faculties operating. Their eyesight and hearing are keen, and they can run about as soon as their downy coats are dry. Light buff in color, with a spotting of dark brown, they match the sun-dappled leaves of the forest floor.

These downy motes of life make good use of their camouflage, "freezing" when threatened so they vanish from view. Or if an enemy pounces in their midst they dash to the nearest shelter—a stick, a clod of earth, or even a dry leaf—and scuttle under it, out of sight.

A few days after hatching, their wing feathers have developed so they can fly. It's an impressive sight to see a dozen piebald chicks, smaller than sparrows, take off into the low branches of a nearby tree. Such an array of tactics is essential to a bird that is sought by almost every predator in the woods.

Now, for this grouse that had shattered my window, the perilous trail had ended. Gently stroking the limp form, I marveled at its warm brown-black-white coloration. I stretched out the sturdy wings that could rocket that two-pound body into booming flight in an instant. I marveled at its henlike bill and feet, just right for picking buds off trees and scratching in the leaves.

A look at those feet showed me how the grouse had been preparing for winter. Along the sides of each toe were small comblike fringes. If the bird had lived, the fringes would have grown larger until they doubled the area of the foot. These "snowshoes" would have allowed it to walk in the loose snow, producing those one-in-front-of-the-other tracks I'd seen so often beneath our spruces.

The grouse had also been in the process of putting on its winter underwear. At the base of each feather was a second feather—fluffy, curled, heat-retaining. The feathers were growing down along its shins, too. Thus it would have had leggings as well.

Although this ruffed grouse had lost its life, I knew its passing would ease the pressure on the food supply of the others it had left behind. Winter is a bottleneck, and the fewer individual creatures there are to squeeze through that bottleneck, the better all around. This brings up another theory about "crazy flight": no matter what the immediate cause, it may be a very practical way to keep the grouse population within limits.

Migration, snowshoes, dull colors, a double suit of feathers—all are declarations by the birds that the cold season is coming. There is yet another avian pronouncement. If you stroll through the woods around Thanksgiving time you may hear it taking place above your head. A soft, steady hammering tells you that a woodpecker is at work.

Chipping away at the rotting wood of the underside of a sloping stub, the bird excavates a cozy home. There it can take shelter through the bitter storms to come. Or, if it builds in a vertical limb, an unerring sixth sense leads it to choose the eastern side, away from the raging nor'westers that often bring our worst blizzards.

The trees and shrubs themselves, apparently insensate as the sun retreats a couple of minutes earlier each day, are undergoing a change. The fading daylight and the falling thermometer cause the plants and trees to go through a process known as "hardening off." Daily they become more calloused to the effects of cold. It's a rapid change, sometimes taking place in a week or two, but it's vital.

A twig can whip about for days in gale winds at thirty below zero with no harm after it has hardened. On the other hand, if you pick the same twig after if has lost its leaves but before it has become fully prepared, the ten-degree temperature of the ice-cube compartment in your refrigerator may be fatal to it in fifteen minutes.

Although plants harden off without any outward sign, there are other changes that are more apparent. Herbaceous perennials that have remained green through those first frosts shrink back to the basic rosette of leaves that will last them through the winter. The withered leaf-stems of burdock and agrimony and beggar's tick drop away, leaving the prickly seed heads exposed and ready to catch in the fur of a passing animal. There they'll remain until the animal scratches them out. They may even ride along all winter until the hair is shed in the spring.

The seed spire of the common dock stands straight and tall, and the ruptured capsules of milkweed expose their loose, fluffy parachute-seeds, like a pillow losing its stuffing. They are ready for the gales of winter, essential in scattering their kind to a new birthplace downwind.

Thus begins the time of the dry plants. All growth that has gone before has been merely a preparation for the slow harvest of this coming season. The leaves and flowers that bloomed have handed over the momentous task of carrying on the species to these dry, brown seeds. The plants will stand there, staunch against the weather, filling their little niche in the snow so their descendents may stand in the sun.

Pokeberry, sumac, rose hips, and highbush cranberry rise above the fallen vegetation. There they await the attention of winter birds. Their flinty seeds, passing through the digestive tract unharmed, will eventually be deposited, complete with a little pat of fertilizer, to germinate with the warmth of spring. Just as with the dried seed heads that remain beyond autumn, winter is a necessary part of their lives. They stand there now, ready for the hungry animals and the blustery, friendly gales.

Although at first glance the evergreens may look the same as on a summer day, they, too, are poised to take advantage of the cold. The cones of many hang in readiness, waiting for alternate freezing and thawing to cause their scales to open and close like venetian blinds. This action helps to liberate their winged seeds, a few at a time. The winds will thin out their foliage, too, so old needles can be replaced in spring by new growth. Broad-leaved evergreens such as laurel and rhododendron draw their leaves closer to the twig now, as if they were huddling to get warm. Thus they prepare against excessive moisture loss.

The deciduous trees and bushes, whose stark outlines are etched against the wintry landscape, need a defense against an ever-present threat during the months to come —the danger of drying. With much of the soil water locked in the frozen ground, there is little chance to replenish loss of moisture. So those buds and twigs and branches have developed a number of methods of conserving water.

Many twigs exude a waxy substance that effectively seals the lenticels, or pores in the bark. Box elder and raspberry twigs have a "bloom"—a waxy powder that can be rubbed off with the finger. In some plants the bloom wears off slowly during the winter. Thus the lenticels are ready to renew their task of exchanging gas and moisture when spring warms the land.

Other twigs, like those of some apples and oaks, are clothed in a velvety fuzz. This fuzz acts as a minuscule windbreak, tempering the force of the drying winds so that a thrashing gale is cut to a zephyr in a fiftieth of an inch. Some plants have excrescences of the bark itself— the euonymus, for instance, with "wings" projecting from the twig as much as an inch. These interfere with airflow, causing a "burble," or eddy of air that creates a protective pneumatic jacket around the branch.

Currant twigs have a bark that peels away in several layers. The outer layer or two forms a papery shield, protecting the tissues beneath. Some grape and blackberry canes sacrifice their entire upper tip, dying back a few feet to a more sheltered portion of the plant.

Buds have protective devices of their own. Most of them are encased in tough, impervious scales. Some, like the buds of willow, are also closely appressed to the twig so they look like mere swellings along the branch. Thus they are protected from the weather. Elm buds are set in a notch partly rimmed by the swollen base of the old leaf. There are fuzzy buds, powdery buds, and tuberculous buds to rival the warts of a toad.

The buds of a certain poplar exude a gummy, sweet-smelling resin, from which we get the Balm-of-Gilead of commerce. This resin prevents the loss of moisture. It also guards against the seepage of rainwater into the loose-fitting scales. Water in a bud, freezing and thawing, would force the scales open or even break them off completely.

The bud that seems prepared against all eventualities, however, is that of the horse chestnut. This tree is closely allied to the buckeye, Ohio's state tree. Its buds are impressive—sometimes as large as the last joint of your little finger. We studied them in high school biology class, as have millions of students through the years. Our source of supply was a beleaguered tree that was annually divested of every bud worthy of the name.

The central growing point of the horse chestnut bud is a complete miniature branch. Telescoped into half an inch is an abbreviated twig, complete with partly-formed leaves. In many cases there is even a cluster of tiny green jewels—the nucleus of next spring's panicle of showy flowers.

Enveloping these tender organs is a thick insulating blanket of cottony cellulose. This, in turn, is encased in tough leathery scales. And, as if that were not enough, the whole is coated with a layer of sticky varnish. So the bud is protected by three separate lines of defense: blanket, scales, and varnish.

The horse chestnut bud typifies, in a way, the world of plants and animals now, when existence seems at its lowest ebb. Apparently devoid of life, it bears the promise of the good, green earth of tomorrow.

So the buds wear their winter jackets and the birds fly south. The wood borer lays up a supply of antifreeze and the woodchuck lies down to sleep. The weasel dons an ermine coat and the white-footed mouse deposits cherry pits in the stocking bag in our cabin.

We never found the missing silk stockings, by the way. Their unknown fate is just a small part of the fascinating business of getting ready for winter. Besides, even though occasional hardy guests use the cabin when the snows are deep, none of them would have planned on using the silk stockings, anyway.

8

Last Call

IF that tadpole had headed for its winter quarters sooner, it might have lived longer.

Not that tadpoles actually hibernate, to be sure. But they become less active as the water cools down. Then when the pond ices over, they sink to the bottom and lie there for hours, or even days, without moving. Silt and floating debris may settle on their fat little bodies until they appear like clods of mud.

That is what ordinarily happens. The tadpole of this beaver pond, however, was different. It was still sculling itself slowly along beneath the clear ice as Peg and I went out looking for a Christmas tree. We paused to consider that fragment of life stubbornly resisting winter, a few inches beneath our feet.

The tadpole drifted over to the edge of a bubble that lay beneath the ice like a huge amoeba. There it gulped a fresh supply of air. And it was at the edge of that bubble that the tadpole's luck ran out.

As we watched, a mahogany-brown shape detached itself from an underwater twig. It was a predaceous Dytiscid beetle, of the general dimensions of a prune pit. It, too, was prolonging its waking life as much as possible before finally burrowing into the mud. Now it drove with powerful strokes of its oarlike legs toward the tadpole.

Ordinarily the tadpole would have wriggled away like a fish. Now, however, those stiff muscles would hardly respond. If I'd had the chance I could have caught it easily in my hand. The only thing that saved the tadpole from instant capture was that the beetle was chilled, too. What started as a devastating rush subsided into dogged pursuit.

We watched the nightmarish chase. It went on for about two yards, with hunter and hunted in slow motion beneath our feet. The tadpole would have won its freedom, yet, out in the open water. Even hampered by the cold, it was faster than the beetle, but in its haste it ran up into the shallows. When it attempted to turn and backtrack, the beetle was waiting.

In an instant the tadpole was seized in a steely embrace. It struggled a moment and then fell limp as its captor bit some vital organ. A single little bubble—perhaps the same gulp of air that had cost the tadpole its life—escaped to the undersurface of the ice.

The scales had come to rest. What the tadpole had lost, the Dytiscid had gained. Its unexpected fortune might be just enough to give it strength to last through the winter. Then it would reappear in the spring, ready to bedevil more tadpoles and fish and other water creatures. It would benefit them, too, in helping keep their numbers within bounds.

Not all late-retiring insects are as fortunate in their search for a livelihood as that beetle. But the drive that seems a part of the act of living keeps a number of them going. Midges and gnats continue to fly over swampy areas until the ground freezes so solid that they cannot make their daily trek out into the weak winter sun. Then, wings folded and legs tight against their bodies, they drop down among the ice crystals, to lie unmoving until spring.

The outer surface of a decaying stump, especially in a sheltered spot, will be decorated with a few insects and mites and spiders on almost any day you care to look for them. And the irrespressible common cricket, given half a chance, keeps right on chirping in a corner of the basement of your home or apartment building. He'll sing all winter, if possible, unless his rendition is cut short by a tone-deaf janitor or a marauding cat.

The most accomplished insomniacs however, are the honeybees. Visit a hive on the coldest day, when your breath freezes on your lips so you can feel little fleeting needles that form as you exhale. Place your ear against the hive and you may hear a distinct humming—the thrilling monotone of life, as a loose ball of insects keeps itself warm by the constant vibration of thousands of wings.

A sudden turn in the weather may bring those durable laborers out for a brief airing. Sometimes they discover sap oozing from a winter-broken branch. Taking advantage of a mild day to gather a few milligrams of sugar, they fly a number of trips between the tree and the hive as if it were July instead of January.

Unseen in the ground, multitudes of hardy inhabitants keep going as long as possible. Last Christmas we were given a pot containing four poinsettia plants. They seemed crowded, so we decided to repot them. I took a pail and shovel to a sheltered spot by a big rock near the spring where we get our water. There, I knew, the sun's warmth kept the soil near the rock from freezing. Sinking the shovel in the ground I came up with a spadeful of earth. When I tumbled it into the pail I noticed an earthworm, looking very pink and healthy despite the frigid soil.

This started me thinking. Back at the house we spread the soil out on newspapers all over the kitchen table. Then we tallied the population of this chilly community. Result: Eight earthworms, two centipedes, five wireworms, five ground beetles, one beetle grub, one cutworm, three millipedes, and perhaps two dozen mites. Roughly fifty inhabitants big enough to be seen with the naked eye in a pailful of earth—all alive and awake on New Year's Day, 1972. A magnifying glass, doubtless, would have allowed us to triple that number.

The food factor may be as important as the chill factor in determining how an animal reacts to the increasing cold. If a warm-blooded creature such as a bird can find enough food, the cold doesn't seem important. I often marvel that a half-ounce chickadee with a body temperature of a hundred degrees can exist, separated from the thirty-below blasts by only a quarter inch of feathers. But exist it does, and in obvious high spirits, too.

Sometimes, either because of a bountiful food supply or because of an injury that kept it from migrating, a summer bird may remain with us all winter. A friend of mine who manages one of Vermont's ski areas showed me where the overflow from the heated pool ran off onto the ground. A patch of bare earth, roughly half the length of a bowling alley, surrounded the steamy trickle of water that flowed out into the snow like a hot spring. And there was a woodcock, walking along through his tiny patch of summer. Occasionally the chunky brown bird with the long beak would do a little shuffle with those sturdy feet.

This, we knew, was his way of calling his food to the surface—the earthworms that apparently mistook the vibration for the drumming of rain.

Over the years we've tallied a number of birds that have stayed beyond their time. On a year-end walk last winter, we saw a gray bird a little smaller than a robin as it perched in a bush over a culvert. The culvert held a stream that flowed all winter from a spring-fed swamp across the road. As we watched, the bird drifted down, snatched a couple of midges flying in the shelter of the culvert, and resumed its place in the bush. The bird was a phoebe—two months and two thousand miles out of place.

Probably some disability had prevented it from migrating in October. And yet there's the chance that this bonanza of a continual supply of insects was too good for the flycatcher to pass up. A friend of mine tells of a Baltimore oriole that ate suet and fruit at her feeder all winter near Boston, and there's seldom a bird walk any time of the year that doesn't produce a robin or two.

Then there was Thurber. We gave this name to a brown thrasher shortly after we'd discovered him huddled in our barn during the big Christmas snowstorm of 1967. All his kind had left New England months before, and he was obviously some sort of holdover.

We brought Thurber into the house and turned him loose. There was nothing wrong with his flying ability that we could see, and he quickly took up residence in the little indoor garden in our bay window. There he gained strength on cranberries, raisins, and a few worms I found for him.

A brown thrasher is hardly an indoor bird, but we couldn't consign him to the bitter cold of midwinter, either. Something had to be done. But what? A friend of ours, a feature writer for a local newspaper, came to the rescue. Why not tell of Thurber's plight and see if the readers had any suggestions?

So, the next day, there was Thurber on page one. Did anybody have any ideas as to what to do with a bird you couldn't keep—and couldn't let go, either?

The story was hardly three hours old when our telephone rang. It was a lady from Burlington. She and her husband planned to jet down to Florida the next morning. If we could get Thurber to them they'd be glad to take him along. They could let him go when they landed.

We found a cat-carrying case made of heavy black cardboard. It would be perfect for the bird, as he'd remain quiet in its darkened interior. So Mr. and Mrs. Jack Gladstone walked up that gangplank with two pieces of hand luggage: Mrs. Gladstone's pocketbook and Mr. Gladstone's "cat."

Three days later a post card showed up in our windswept mailbox. "Thurber went with the wind," it said. "And were all the passengers surprised when we got off the plane, opened the box, and let out a bird!"

In about a week the box was returned. Inside, we found a single slip of paper, with a sketch of a bird's foot and the single word: "Thanks." So for one bird that missed the boat, so to speak, all was not lost. He merely hopped a plane.

Man's gadgetry often helps birds in another way. One place to look for tardy migrants is on the arms of a television antenna. Not that the gleaming metal offers much solace to an out-of-season bird, but its location makes it attractive. A handy place to mount an antenna is on the chimney of a house, and the draft of the chimney rises and surrounds the birds with a warm, if smelly, flood of air. A friend even swears that a flock of starlings loved to ride her antenna as she turned the rotor. But I believe they just allowed it to bring them around to where the air was warmest.

Sometimes the birds will even perch directly on the chimney itself. Under the spell of such inducements, plus the lure of the proliferating birdfeeder, it's hardly surprising that our Christmas bird count in 1971 produced fifty-seven species of birds—nearly two dozen of them left over from the long departed summer.

One other bird refuses to yield to the snow and ice. It is a creature that has existed in mythology since the time of the ancient Greeks. Known in folklore as the halcyon, it is supposed to be a bird markedly like our kingfisher. For reasons known only to itself it chooses these last few days of the year as the time to build its nest.

Gifted with power over the wind and the waves, the halcyon speaks the word—and the winter seas become calm. The bitter gales cease their raging. The very sun stands still. Gently alighting on the surface of the ocean, the legendary bird builds its nest on the water and lays its eggs. During the two or three weeks of incubation the weather holds itself in check. Then, when the young of the halcyon are safely fledged, the storms descend once more.

A fabrication, of course, but the legend has at least a partial basis in fact. This is the time of the winter solstice —meaning "sun standing still," to translate the words literally. Lingering on the far horizon the sun does, indeed, seem to remain in one small segment of the sky. Actually, this is because our northern hemisphere is reaching the end of its farthest slant away from the sun and its orbit is just beginning to bring it back toward the summer position, six months away. So, like a pendulum that comes to a pause in its swing for a moment before it starts back, the earth and its sun seem to hang suspended.

Today we still refer to calm weather as "halcyon days," although we may allude as much to the days of summer as winter. And even in our enlightened twentieth century we hearken back to the age-old myth as we repeat the scientific name of the kingfisher: *Megaceryle alcyon*, "the large halcyon."

As if there was a further grain of truth to the legend, an occasional kingfisher may remain through the winter near a waterfall. There, perching on an overhanging branch, it scans the river for a trout or dace or minnow. Plummeting down through the icy spray, the bird careens into the water. Rising, it shakes the glittering drops from its plumage as it bears its prize aloft. And since the kingfisher nests in a hidden tunnel in the river bank, the secrecy surrounding its family life could well have narrowed the credibility gap between fact and fable.

Halcyon days or not, the kingfisher's searching gaze may alight on another creature reluctant to retire for the winter. We see his tracks on the snow of our bridge almost any morning until the river has frozen to a faint murmur beneath a bumpy avenue of ice. Our year-ender is the common raccoon, still snooping about with that boundless curiosity, as long as the watercourses remain open. Puddling through the mud with his black paws, he may catch a groggy salamander or a drowsy frog. Then, apparently because of the feel of the object under those sensitive fingers, he proceeds to souse his meal thoroughly in the chilly stream—even if it is a fish that has been in water all its life.

An occasional skunk still putters around the back yard and along the edge of our woods. Like the raccoon, the skunk is an opportunist. It may keep prowling for edibles until the snow is so deep that it cannot travel. If the snow cover is scant and the cold not too severe, skunks and raccoons may reappear every week or so all winter. Then, some January morning, you speculate about the marauder who scattered your garbage bag all over the back yard. Was he poking around because he hadn't yet retired for the winter, or because he was getting a start on the new year? Or was he just suffering from insomnia?

Our graceful woodland neighbor, the deer, is putting the finishing touches on its wanderings for the year, too. As long as the snow is shallow we can see the deer at the edges of woods and out in the fields, nipping the tops of alfalfa and other low-growing greenery.

When the storms rage in earnest, however, the deer disappears until spring. Retiring to the sheltered forest thickets—of white cedar, its favorite winter browse, if possible—the deer joins with others of its kind in a cold-weather "yard." There it wanders about, keeping the snow tramped down as it roams in a search for food.

A deer yard may cover an area the size of a baseball diamond, or it may equal the expanse of several football fields. As the snow deepens, the deer keep certain paths open. They plod along these paths from one thicket of edible browse to another. The snow builds up beneath their feet, raising them so they can reach ever higher after the twigs and buds. As food becomes more scarce, they stand on their hind legs, stretching as high as they can reach. During a severe winter, they may take every bud and twig to a height of five or six feet, thus leaving a "browse line" below which the trees and bushes are bare of foliage.

Deer, along with many other cloven-hoofed animals such as cows and sheep, have no front teeth in the upper jaw. There is, however, a tough pad of tissue against which the lower teeth can bite. The tongue of a deer is prehensile, grasping a few twigs like an encircling hand and pressing them against the pad, aided by the lower teeth. Then, with a motion of the head the twigs are torn from the parent branch. Hence the shrubbery where a deer has been feeding will show frayed and broken ends —in contrast to the neatly clipped stubs left by rabbits, squirrels, and mice with their opposing sets of sharp incisors. In addition, rodents and rabbits usually turn their heads sideways to nip a twig, so the cuts are slanted, as with a knife.

One of the late-season foods of many forest animals at this time is itself a holdover from summer that keeps going until the final freeze-up. This is the oyster mushroom, an odd fanlike structure that appeared in September on the sides of dying trees.

There are several species of this fungus. It receives its name from the habit of growing in ascending ranks, like oysters on a piling. Protruding from the bark further each day during the fall, the stemless oyster mushroom releases a slow shower of powdery spores from gills on its underside. The spores are produced constantly, often sifting down onto the top of the mushroom beneath, or swirling up on rising air to cover the upper skin of their own parent mushroom. When snow comes they may darken its surface like smoke.

We keep on the lookout for these last of the edible fungi. There's an old elm stub near the campus of Middlebury College that has provided a crop of the elm mushrooms for several years. A deceased maple in Lincoln is just as faithful with its particular species. Either type, with its buffy fans and firm white inner flesh, is far more tasty than the pallid parasols offered at fancy prices in the supermarket. So, as long as the oyster mushrooms brave the icy blasts—which may be almost into January —we can buy a pound of hamburg at the local market and then swing around past the old maple for the rest of the meal.

Other never-say-die plants add their bit to these closing days of the year. They carry their own silent struggles to the last: the forgotten, forlorn dandelion that, as one naturalist puts it, "gilds both edges of the year," and the tiny chickweed that may put out a hopeful white blossom on your lawn, even under the snow. The remains of the last green tops in your vegetable garden still mark the summer rows, and if you forget to pull up your onions they may poke tentative green fingers up through the rubble long after the rest of your garden is harvested.

One plant that constantly surprises me on these frosty days is a species whose name suggests the lush, humid warmth of summer. It is a true orchid, first cousin of those colorful blooms that grow in such profusion in the tropics. Looked at with a magnifying glass, its delicate white blossoms are as lovely as those found in any corsage. Yet here it is, its dozen or so tiny flowers arranged in a double spiral on a six-inch stalk—the ladies tresses orchid, one of the last flowering meadow plants, sometimes poking incongruously up through an early snowfall.

Even after the ground is frozen and ice has formed on the ponds, its blossoms may remain. They turn brown so slowly that it's hard to tell when the plant is really dead. A few last insects, apparently attracted by some lingering scent, clamber over it until the snows of winter finally cover them all.

I always enjoy seeing the pumpkins at this time of the year. Not the round, bright orange spheres of a few months ago, but the jack-o-lanterns left over from the night of the goblins and witches. Forgotten on front steps of houses, the Halloween pranksters yield to a devastating old age. The crafty eyes droop until they're doleful. The wicked leer subsides into a wrinkle, and those horrendous fangs become bumps in the now toothless gums. Finally, with a sigh of resignation under the weight of the snow bonnets they wear, the castaways collapse into a heap of compost.

Drowsy pumpkins, obstinate mushrooms, birds that refuse to migrate, and animals that won't go to sleep—these are the rear guard of the old year as it wobbles to its finish. They are, in a way, Mother Nature in the process of closing up for the winter, slamming a door, shutting a window, pulling a dust cloth over the furniture. Soon the place will be closed for keeps.

But sometimes, even as you slam one door, another flies open. And this is just what happened on Saturday morning, January 8, 1972, as Peg and I were snowshoeing with a neighbor in the deep woods five miles from our home. The sun was bright, but the temperature was well below zero and the frost crystals sparkled in the calm air above the mountain stream whose waters had not yet frozen over. It was one of those splendid days when the crunch of the snowshoes and the joy of living were all anyone would ever wish.

But there was yet to be more. I left the other two and struggled down a steep bank to a swampy area. Once at the bottom I looked idly around—and found myself a spectator at what might be called a woodland relay race.

There were the two team members, successful in their struggle against time: a witch hazel bush from the old year and a pussy willow symbolizing the new. Both were in bloom, and, with a little imagination, one could picture the spark of life passing from the former to the latter.

I inspected the witch hazel—the last of the year's common shrubs to put forth blossoms. Its flowers are peculiar structures, with spidery yellow petals half an inch long. They spread themselves out to the winter sun long after most other buds are securely wrapped for the season. Apparently the visits of a few hardy insects and the assistance of the winter gales are enough to pollinate these maverick blossoms.

The pussy willow, with those first silvery-soft catkins, was also bidding for those insects and winter gales—or for their successors in the days to follow. Old and new, within arm's reach of each other.

I picked a sprig of each plant and continued on a great circle toward my starting point. When the three of us got together I asked Peg what they had seen.

"Not much," she said. "A few tracks, that's all. Fox and red squirrel and snowshoe hare tracks. And the usual chickadees and woodpeckers."

With an air of elaborate carelessness, I produced the branches I'd been hiding behind my back. "Nothing else?" I asked. "No year end specials or sneak previews?"

They admired the two-twig bouquet. Then, back at the car, we jotted down the signs of the seasons we had seen in our two hours on snowshoes. When we finished our list there was one bird we had to record with a question mark. It had been in the top of an old spruce by the beaver dam.

"We're not sure what it was," Peg recalled. "It was silhouetted against the sky, but seemed to be gray and black. We saw it for only a second before it flew away."

We considered the possibilities. The bird could have been a Canada jay; they occasionally follow the mountains south from Quebec. It could have been a tufted titmouse; they've been working farther north into Vermont each year. Or it could have been a lone northern shrike—headed north or south. Only a few more weeks remained before the anniversary of that other shrike that had visited our front yard on a day in February.

So we compromised on "northern shrike, possible" as our only entry in the column reserved for spring birds, and hoped we had guessed correctly. As we headed for home, we decided our hunch had been right. It *had* been a northern shrike and he was, indeed, returning north for the spring.

Or at least he could have been. Like the rest of his woodland neighbors, he had little respect for the calendar anyway.